II0639087

SHORT-TERM
SPIRITUAL GUIDANCE

CREATIVE PASTORAL CARE AND COUNSELING SERIES
Howard W. Stone, Editor

Crisis Counseling (revised edition) by Howard W. Stone

Integrative Family Therapy by David C. Olsen

Counseling Men by Philip L. Culbertson

Woman-Battering by Carol J. Adams

Counseling Adolescent Girls by Patricia H. Davis

Cross-Cultural Counseling by Aart M. van Beek

Creating a Healthier Church by Ronald W. Richardson

Grief, Transition, and Loss by Wayne E. Oates

When Faith Is Tested by Jeffry R. Zurheide

Competency-Based Counseling by Frank Thomas and Jack Cockburn

Pastoral Care of Older Adults by Harold G. Koenig and Andrew J. Weaver

The Pastor as Moral Guide by Rebekah L. Miles

Premarital Guidance by Charles W. Taylor

Pastoral Care of Gays, Lesbians, and Their Families by David K. Switzer

Pastoral Visitation by Nancy J. Gorsuch

Pastoral Care Emergencies by David K. Switzer

Short-Term Spiritual Guidance by Duane R. Bidwell

CREATIVE PASTORAL CARE AND COUNSELING

SHORT-TERM
SPIRITUAL GUIDANCE

DUANE R. BIDWELL

FORTRESS PRESS   MINNEAPOLIS

SHORT-TERM SPIRITUAL GUIDANCE

Copyright © 2004 Augsburg Fortress. All rights reserved. Except for brief quotations in critical articles or reviews, no part of this book may be reproduced in any manner without prior written permission from the publisher. Write: Permissions, Augsburg Fortress, Box 1209, Minneapolis, MN 55440.

Cover art © Photodisc, Inc.

Scripture quotations are from the New Revised Standard Version Bible, copyright © 1989 by the Division of Christian Education of the National Council of the Churches of Christ in the USA, and are used by permission.

Material in chapter 9 was previously published in Duane R. Bidwell and Lee Self, "Brief Encounters: What Spiritual Directors Can Learn from the Short-Term Therapy Model," *Presence: The Journal of Spiritual Directors International* 8:2 (2002): 20–32.

ISBN 0-8006-3658-9

The paper used in this publication meets the minimum requirements of American National Standard for Information Sciences—Permanence of Paper for Printed Library Materials, ANSI Z329.48-1984.

Manufactured in the U.S.A.

08	07	06	05	04	1	2	3	4	5	6	7	8	9	10

To Lynn and Thich Phap Nhan,
my first directors

CONTENTS

EDITOR'S FOREWORD

Before I had a chance to talk with Duane Bidwell, I assumed that all spiritual direction was long-term; I figured that my brief work with three different directors in three different parts of the country was atypical, that perhaps I had not had the real thing. I gained from each experience of spiritual direction—life changing in some respects—but possibly it was not what it should have been but merely a watered-down version.

In *Short-Term Spiritual Guidance*, Bidwell exposes the myth that most care for the spirit occurs as a long-term process. He points out that with the exception of the full-time religious, historically most spiritual direction has been brief—a matter of a few sessions and, indeed, sometimes only one session.

Bidwell recognizes that most people neither have nor take the time to engage in a long series of spiritual direction sessions. He conceives that most direction offered in the context of the parish or the hospital consists, at most, of five sessions or fewer.

Bidwell also points out that most individuals who seek care do not go because they are required to by their religious order or because they want a lifelong companion with whom to begin a journey of spiritual growth. Rather, most who seek spiritual care today do so because they have had a recent experience that they want to make sense of or because they are experiencing a difficulty or a crisis in their spiritual life on which they want to gain some perspective. *Short-Term Spiritual Guidance* recognizes the context within which most spiritual direction originates.

Years ago, when I began reading in the area of spiritual direction, I found one thing missing in most of the literature: there were few specifics about how you go about the task and few descriptions of specific interventions that could be used. This book fills that void. Bidwell offers several specific interventions that the reader can use when caring for the spiritual life. He not only makes the point that, historically, most spirit care is brief but also goes on to suggest how brief spiritual direction can be done. He provides a way that ministers and concerned laypersons can offer spiritual direction that honors the person, recognizes the context of how the care is offered "on the run," and stays true to the historical ways spiritual direction has been offered. I think you will find his specific suggestions for how to go about care, and the specific interventions involved, very beneficial.

Bidwell creatively uses theory from brief pastoral counseling and brief psychotherapy to make clear a particular style of spiritual direction that does not relinquish the basic purposes and goals of spiritual direction yet makes such direction much more effective for both the pastoral caregiver and the person receiving care who are not in a position to form longer-term relationships.

I am confident that reading this book will strengthen and enrich your spiritual direction, pastoral care, counseling, and general ministry. Bidwell brings to his work the wisdom gained through many years offering and teaching about spiritual direction, both in the parish and as a seminary professor. The scope and quality of the care you offer to others will surely benefit from his knowledge and sound guidance.

HOWARD W. STONE

PREFACE

Although thoroughly informed by the classic Christian spiritual traditions, this book represents a significant departure from most contemporary writing about spiritual direction. The distinction is most evident in its "starting assumptions"—assumptions about the book's audience, about the "typical" experience of spiritual direction in the American parish, about the value of concrete interventions in spiritual direction, about how a spiritual director ought to behave during a spiritual direction conversation, and about what constitutes an appropriate theoretical foundation for spiritual direction.

First, the book conceives its primary audience as parish pastors, chaplains, seminarians, and others who provide spiritual guidance "on the run." For these readers, spiritual direction is a small part of a busy, multifaceted ministry. As a result, these readers need skills and techniques designed for brief encounters in addition to training best suited to long-term spiritual direction relationships.

Second, the book assumes that much (if not most) contemporary spiritual direction takes place in fewer than five meetings. In contrast, most spiritual direction texts assume a long-term relationship in which weekly or monthly appointments, spread over the course of a year or longer, are the norm. One contemporary author even suggests ten sessions are necessary simply to hear a person's story and evaluate whether she is fit for spiritual direction in the first place!

Few parish pastors (and few parishioners), however, have or take the time for this sort of formal, ongoing conversation about an individual's spiritual life. Rather, the pastor and parishioner meet two or three times to address a specific question, to make sense of certain experiences, or to resolve a particular spiritual crisis. These meetings are opportunities to help people learn to listen *on their own and with others* for God's presence, without the guidance of a pastor or chaplain.

This method of practicing spiritual guidance is in some ways a return to the Protestant tradition of spiritual direction developed during and after the Reformation. Early Protestant spiritual directors, as described by Kenneth Leech, claimed little authority in relation to their directees, perceived the direction relationship as temporary, and tended to focus on crisis resolution rather than on lifelong companionship on a person's journey with God.[1] This is the spirit in which I have written *Short-Term Spiritual Guidance*.

Third, the book offers concrete interventions that directors may use to enhance the spiritual growth and maturity of directees. These interventions—often missing from contemporary spiritual direction texts—are drawn both from the Christian spiritual traditions and from the practice of brief pastoral counseling. They are intended as a supplement to—not a replacement for—the hard work of listening and discernment that forms the backbone of quality spiritual direction.

Fourth, the book encourages the director to take an active stance with directees by questioning, coaching, and shaping the conversation in deliberate ways. This contrasts with the almost passive stance advocated by some contemporary texts on spiritual direction, which promote reflective listening within a Rogerian, "client-directed" approach as the director's primary orientation toward the person seeking direction.

Silence and reflective listening are essential to quality spiritual direction, but they should not serve as the director's only tools, especially when direction consists of two or three meetings. Practitioners of brief spiritual direction must learn to be both active *and* contemplative, an idea affirmed by Christian spiritual traditions.

Fifth, the book is grounded in the theory and practice of brief psychotherapy and brief pastoral counseling. These disciplines provide practical and clinically effective methods for short-term care. But these methods are quite different from long-term approaches to healing conversation, which tend to be shaped by the psychoanalytic and depth psychologies that provide the psychological foundation for most contemporary spiritual direction texts.

In keeping with the theory of brief pastoral counseling, this book focuses on what is already going well in an individual's life with God as a basis for future growth. Thus, the text prepares caregivers to make the most of brief encounters by teaching them to focus on how God is *already active* in the directee's life. This allows directors and directees to identify God's action and to respond in ways that collaborate with God's intention for the directee.

A dual focus on *identifying God's action* and *discerning an appropriate response* is central to all spiritual direction, whether long-term or short-term. The difficulty is that most training programs assume a long-term orientation, failing to prepare trainees for the reality of short-term encounters. This establishes a dichotomy between theory, which focuses on long-term relationships, and the actual practice of spiritual direction, which is frequently short-term. This dichotomy can be confusing, because many trained directors simply are not equipped to deal with the short-term spiritual direction relationships common in our culture. Yet most directors are quick to affirm the value of even a single meeting between a director and a directee.

Members of the spiritual direction community in the United States tend to be tolerant and supportive of one another, but I suspect many spiritual directors will meet this text with skepticism and perhaps some criticism. The model of spiritual direction promoted here may appear goal-directed and task-driven when compared to the dominant model of spiritual direction in the United States. Certainly, the approach I advocate has a strong counseling bias that is sometimes rejected in the literature of spiritual direction, and it may appear to some to be direction by the numbers rather than by prayerful discernment.

I acknowledge these criticisms and share some of them. But I believe the model of spiritual direction presented in *Short-Term Spiritual Guidance* takes seriously the context in which many pastors, chaplains, and other spiritual guides practice their art. Brief spiritual direction will not be appropriate for all situations, but it will be for many.

No book grows from an author's isolated mind. In fact, the phrase "isolated mind" is itself an oxymoron; writing and thinking always take place in the context of community. Many people and experiences have contributed to this work. My thanks (and a deep bow of respect) go first to the many individuals who have allowed me to walk with them as their spiritual director (and taught me much) in the last fifteen years. Thanks also to Howard Stone, editor of the Creative Pastoral Care and Counseling series at Fortress Press, who first proposed this text; Michael West and Beth Wright, my editors at Fortress Press; Margie Atkinson, Linda Ford, Katherine Godby, and Rich Rathbun, colleagues in the Ph.D. seminar at Brite Divinity School, where this line of inquiry began; John Mabry, former editor of *Presence: The Journal of Spiritual Directors International*, and to the journal's anonymous peer reviewers who have commented on this approach to spiritual direction; J. F. Wickey and Sara Tinsley, for help with manuscript preparation; and the congregations in Texas that nourished me as a pastor, spiritual director, and pastoral counselor: First Christian Church in Granbury, First Presbyterian Church in Bonham, First Presbyterian Church in Bridgeport, Lien Hoa Buddhist Temple in Irving, Oak Hill Presbyterian Church in Fort Worth, St. Philip Presbyterian Church in Hurst, and St. Stephen Presbyterian

Church in Fort Worth. Finally, my deepest love and gratitude to Karee Galloway, my friend and spouse, and to our son, Ben Thu Ngoc Bidwell (who, at two years old, is a far better spiritual director than his father ever hopes to be!).

1

THE MINISTRY
OF SPIRITUAL DIRECTION

Roy wasn't sure why he was lingering outside the pastor's office after church. Worship felt empty to him that morning, and he just needed to connect with someone for a change—to talk about what was going on in his heart rather than pretending everything was fine. When the clot of people had emptied from the hallway and all of the happy families were safely headed to lunch at nearby chain restaurants, Roy tentatively knocked on the minister's door. "Got a minute?" he asked when Pastor Tom invited him in.

"Sure, Roy," Tom said. They settled onto opposite ends of the pastor's sofa. "What's going on?"

"Well," Roy began. "I'm not really sure. I've just had this feeling lately that there's something more to life, something I'm missing."

A torrent of words followed. Roy described the empty, restless feeling he faced daily despite a full social calendar, success as an attorney, volunteer work at the church, and a growing relationship with someone he could imagine loving all his life.

"I'm not really sure why I'm here," he finished. "I just thought you could help me figure out what's going on."

Hundreds of pastoral care encounters begin just this way: a parishioner like Roy brings a vague problem or specific concern to the pastor, who listens actively and compassionately. The pastor draws on her professional training and experience to make herself as helpful as possible. Sometimes, simply listening provides the best possible care; other times, pastoral counseling—skillfully bringing the resources of psychology and spirituality to bear on the situation—best serves the situation. At still other times, however, parishioners want and need *spiritual direction*: intentional listening for and conversation about the presence of God in their lives.

While most forms of pastoral care focus on the *outer* events and relationships of the parishioner's life (for example, coping with the strains of getting older, deciding whether to accept a new job, or dealing with angry teenagers or a loveless marriage), spiritual direction focuses primarily on the parishioner's *inner* relationship with God—a relationship that takes place amid all of life's events and relationships. Thus, spiritual direction serves two purposes: first, identifying how God is present in a person's life (which is always experienced in unique and particular ways), and second, discerning an appropriate response to God's presence and action.

Discerning which form of pastoral care is most appropriate to a given situation is one of a pastor's daily challenges. The theory of brief psychotherapy that informs this book would recommend that parishioners be allowed to decide what pastoral approach would help them most. To find out what approach Roy might find helpful in the opening example, Pastor Tom could summarize the conversation and ask which concern seems most important at the moment. If Roy answers by saying, "The restlessness is really affecting my productivity at work; I've got to find a way to keep it under control," Tom might suggest pastoral counseling. If Roy says, "It all seems equally important; I guess I need to sort through some of this and see if I can understand it better," Tom might choose to employ active, reflective listening as his primary form of care. But if Roy answers by saying, "I really want to understand where God is in all of this," Tom can assume Roy is seeking spiritual direction.

If this were the case, how might Pastor Tom proceed? Let's listen in on the conversation.

LISTENING FOR GLIMMERS OF GOD:
BRIEF SPIRITUAL DIRECTION WITH ROY

Pastor Tom smiled. "That's a good question, Roy: Where is God in all of this? I guess we both start with the assumption that God *is* involved in all of this." Roy nodded. "In the past, you've told me you feel drawn to simple, outdoor prayer, especially in the mountains. And if I remember right, spending time with friends is one important way that you experience God's love for you." Roy nodded again.

"Good," said Tom. "I'm impressed that you know what helps you feel in touch with God. Is that restless feeling there even at those times—when you're alone outdoors or having fun with friends?"

"Yes," Roy said. "I've tried reading the Bible, spending more time with friends, spending less time with friends, asking God for direction. I even tried keeping a journal, like you suggested in your sermon last month. Nothing helps."

"Well," Tom said. "I don't know for sure what's going on, but I'm wondering if the restlessness is a sign that God wants to spend more time with you—time that's different from the way you usually spend time with God."

Roy considered this in silence for a moment. "Could be, I guess," he replied. "What exactly are you suggesting?"

"I don't know for sure," Tom replied. "Let's keep talking and see what emerges. Tell me about a time recently when the restlessness wasn't there, or when it wasn't as strong as usual."

Roy looked out the window. "Well . . . now that I think about it, I guess the restlessness wasn't there last week when our Bible study group made sandwiches for the homeless shelter."

"Really? Tell me more about that—where was God while you were making sandwiches?"

Roy smiled. "God was right there with me. I remember thinking, 'God is feeding the hungry through my hands.' It was a very prayerful feeling; I intentionally focused on God's love as I smeared peanut butter on the bread. And I remember that I wasn't saying anything or even listening to the others while they talked. I was just focused on letting God's love flow through me into the sandwich." He paused. "That sounds kind of weird, doesn't it?"

Tom laughed. "No, not at all! It sounds like a very meaningful time for you—a very prayerful time, as you said. How was it different from your other prayer times?"

"I was *doing* something instead of just sitting quietly," Roy said. "And I was focused on doing something for others. It wasn't just 'me and God' like usual—it was 'me and God and the homeless people.' And now that I remember it, I felt more peaceful right then than I had in weeks. In fact, just remembering it makes me feel more peaceful."

"That's interesting," Tom said. "Any clues in there about how God might want to spend time with you in a way that's different from how you usually do it?"

"There might be some clues," Roy said with a smile. "That feeling of 'me and God and the homeless people' instead of 'me and God' seems important. I guess it would be easy to find out. I could try making sandwiches for the shelter again or I could volunteer someplace for other people and just try to notice God's presence again."

"Seems worth a try," Tom said. "Let me know how it goes."

In just a few minutes of conversation, Tom provided significant spiritual direction to Roy. He used three specific interventions. First, he suggested—and Roy accepted—that the restlessness Roy felt was not a problem but an indication that God wanted to interact with Roy differently. Second, he carefully directed Roy's attention to a time when the restlessness was interrupted by a feeling of God's presence. Together, they explored what that time felt like and what it meant to Roy. Third, Tom helped Roy find a way to respond to God's invitation to spend time together in a different way.

Tom's way of providing care to Roy—walking with him in his experience while gently collaborating in a conversation that allowed Roy to feel less "stuck" in his relationship with God—is at the heart of effective, short-term spiritual direction.

WHAT IS SPIRITUAL DIRECTION?

Entire books have been written about the ministry of spiritual direction—what it is, how it evolved, and how it is practiced. More than a few pages are required to address the complexity of the subject. Thus, this section is not the final word on spiritual direction but provides a summary understanding, painted with broad strokes rather than fine detail.[1] Such a summary serves two purposes. First, it offers an introduction to spiritual direction for those unfamiliar with this ministry. Second, it provides a background for the practice of spiritual direction developed in the rest of the book. The summary includes five parts: a definition of spiritual direction, a history, a discussion of how spiritual direction differs from other forms of pastoral care, a look at what spiritual directors do, and an exploration of characteristics common to effective spiritual direction relationships.

Defining Spiritual Direction

One step toward understanding something is to define it, and there is no shortage of definitions for the term *spiritual direction*. Some definitions focus on the sacramental aspects of the ministry; others, on the interrelationship of director, directee, and God; and still others, on the model used to attend to God's presence. For the purposes of this text, I will work from a definition offered by William A. Barry and William J. Connolly. They state that spiritual direction is

> help given by one Christian to another which enables that person to pay attention to God's personal communication to him or her, to respond to this personally communicating God, to grow in intimacy with this God, and to live out the conse-

quences of the relationship. The *focus* of this type of spiritual direction is on experience, not ideas, and specifically on religious experience, i.e., any experience of the mysterious Other whom we call God.[2]

A History of Spiritual Direction

Historically, the practice of Christian spiritual direction is rooted in the fourth-century deserts of Egypt, Syria, and Palestine. Laymen and laywomen disappointed with urban Christianity went to live alone in the desert, intending to practice the spiritual disciplines that can lead a person to holiness. Other Christians began to recognize the spiritual wisdom and power of these hermits and sought them out for spiritual advice. In the beginning, that advice, or spiritual direction, tended to focus on the "discernment of thoughts"—discovering whether a person's ways of thinking were godly or sinful and then devising ways to resist thoughts that led away from God. The goal of the practice of spiritual direction was an individual's mystical union with God.

This emphasis on discernment and the disclosure of thoughts caused the practice of spiritual direction over time to become intertwined with the practice of confession. Men noted to be full of the Holy Spirit were authorized by bishops to serve as confessors and spiritual directors, contributing to the idea of "the spiritual father," a holy man who was spiritually mature and wise in discernment and who therefore could help others "birth" their spiritual selves and make progress in contemplation. (There were, of course, always "spiritual mothers" as well—women not authorized by the church hierarchy but recognized by the people for their ability to lead others on the spiritual journey.) Gradually, spiritual direction became institutionalized in the church. A final step in this process came with the Rule of Benedict, which establishes the abbot of a monastery as the spiritual director of all monks and laity under his jurisdiction.

In the Western church, particularly the English pastoral tradition, the parish priest provided the primary model for spiritual direction. In this model, spiritual direction had less to do with mystical contemplation or union with God than with ethical and moral guidance. American spiritual direction tended to be influenced by this model, although some argue that in the twentieth century, American spiritual direction distanced itself from the ministry's traditional historical and theological moorings to rely instead on psychology and the personal experiences of those seeking direction.

Distinction from Other Forms of Pastoral Care

It is important to distinguish spiritual direction from other forms of pastoral care. A good way to do so is to look at the purpose of the caring relationship. In other forms of pastoral care, the pastor might seek to provide information about a particular faith tradition, to comfort someone before surgery, to relieve anxiety, to solve family problems, to clarify ethical dilemmas, or to provide companionship. Through God's grace, these sorts of pastoral care may lead a person into a deeper relationship with God. In the ministry of spiritual direction, however, the *primary* purpose of providing care is to deepen a person's relationship with God. Such secondary benefits as relieved anxiety, solved problems, or a greater knowledge about a faith tradition are wonderful, but they are not a focus of the spiritual director's intentional concern.

The practice of spiritual direction happens through careful listening as people describe their experiences of God. At the same time, the spiritual director also listens for how God is present and active during the spiritual direction conversation. This requires the ability to listen *in the moment*, a stance reflected in Jeannette Bakke's suggestion that spiritual directors approach their ministry by saying, "During this time together, I give myself, my awareness and attention, my hopes and heart *to God for you. I surrender myself to God for your sake.* I will listen with one ear to the Holy Spirit and with the other to your description of your prayer and relationship with God. I will support you in prayer as you describe and discern your experiences with God and respond to you out of my ongoing prayer and reflection."[3]

Another way to distinguish spiritual direction from other types of pastoral care is to identify the person's motivation for seeking help. Five areas of concern frequently lead people to seek spiritual direction: union with God, imitation of Christ, methods of prayer and forgiveness, making sense of foundational experiences, and searching for meaning in life.[4] Specific needs within these areas of concern include seeking guidance in spiritual reading, detecting mediocrity or inner weakness, handling dry or difficult prayer, doing penance, discerning vocation, assessing progress in the spiritual life, and receiving support in (and being held accountable for) spiritual practices.[5] People who bring these sorts of concerns or needs to conversation with their pastors may be seeking spiritual direction. Such concerns are excellent reasons to seek spiritual guidance!

Less helpful reasons for seeking spiritual direction also exist. They include a desire for theological knowledge rather than deeper awareness and experience of God's presence, a general yearning for companionship, a more specific yearning for mutual conversation about faith, and a search for a quick and easy cure for life's emotional difficulties. None of these motivations is likely to lead to a satisfying experience for the person seeking spiritual direction or for the person providing it.

What Spiritual Directors Do

Spiritual direction is not a mystical process requiring arcane knowledge or esoteric spiritual formation, but a director does need experience and maturity in the spiritual life. "Hard-headed realism," writes Josef Sudbrack, "not misty-eyed enthusiasm, is the key feature of spiritual guidance."[6] These qualities do not relate to chronological age or academic degrees. Rather, spiritual directors must be people who can sustain relationships and listen well; they must also be people of prayer. Living a spiritual life—let alone guiding someone else—can be confusing and enigmatic. But a director can take comfort in knowing that common sense is the most reliable guide to spiritual growth, especially when coupled with an attitude of acute awareness and openness to the experiences of others and the meanings people give to those experiences.

Listening to how people make sense of their own experiences and discerning how they are called to respond to those experiences are key. A call to action comes from God, not from the directee or the director. A spiritual director does not make decisions or tell people what to do but helps them (in the words of Thomas Merton) "to recognize and to follow the inspirations of grace" in their lives.[7] In a way, the title of spiritual director is a misnomer. The true director is the Holy Spirit; the human director is merely a guide who helps track the Spirit through the landscape of the directees' lives.

That landscape comprises everything that happens to a person. For that reason, spiritual directors work with the stuff of everyday experience: changing diapers, getting along with coworkers, shopping for groceries. But spiritual direction attends to these experiences differently than therapy or counseling does. Therapists and counselors strive to resolve people's problems or at least to help them respond to difficulties in a healthier way. Spiritual directors, on the other hand, focus on helping people discern God's presence in their lives so they might engage in a dialogue with God. Out of this dialogue, they ascertain the most appropriate response to God's action. Simply put, spiritual directors offer assistance to persons in their growing relationship with God.

There is no one model for effective spiritual direction. Different traditions have different understandings of the spiritual direction relationship.

Some emphasize a master-and-disciple relationship between the director and the directee. Others, such as the *staretz* relationship in the Russian Orthodox Church, have an almost shamanistic quality. The ancient Celtic church understood spiritual directors to be companions on the life journey, calling them *anamchara*, which means "soul friend." This book assumes a more mutual, peer-to-peer relationship typical of the relationship between most Anglo, mainstream Protestant pastors and their parishioners.

Elements of an Effective Spiritual Direction Relationship

No matter what model of relationship guides the way spiritual directors and directees work together, effective spiritual direction does have some common elements. The following paragraphs describe four of the many conditions that contribute to successful spiritual direction relationships.

First, good spiritual directors have a certain personal holiness recognized by other people. They are committed to prayer and experienced in its various forms. They receive spiritual direction themselves, and often their practice of spiritual direction is accountable to a supervisor or supervision group.

Second, spiritual direction today is rarely understood as a hierarchical relationship. While the director is recognized as someone with piety, learning, and more (or at least *different*) experience with the ways of God than the directee has, the director is not assumed to be an authority who must be obeyed or to whom a directee must submit. The director has limited authority; effective spiritual direction relationships are marked by a mutuality that includes an intimate bond of love and respect between the people involved. Good directors adopt an attitude of acceptance and support, not one of judgment.

Third, effective spiritual direction is a collaborative effort in which both director and directee seek guidance from the Holy Spirit together. The director serves as a source and catalyst for spiritual growth in the directee, but Christ is the source and goal of the direction process.

Fourth, freedom in the Spirit is the ultimate goal of spiritual direction. Effective spiritual direction relationships increase the freedom of both the person acting as director and the person receiving direction. Spiritual direction relationships that are oppressive or that shut down possibilities are rarely effective.

LONG-TERM VERSUS SHORT-TERM SPIRITUAL DIRECTION

In its monastic forms, spiritual direction was a long-term endeavor. Novices typically would work with a particular director throughout their formation process, which could last for years. Once novices became full members of their orders, these monks and nuns often worked with one director for years (if not for life). In the twentieth century, as psychoanalytic and psychodynamic psychology became influential, spiritual direction relationships outside of monastic communities also became perceived as long-term commitments. Monthly meetings were the norm. As a result, most contemporary training programs for spiritual directors assume that directors and directees will have a long-term relationship. But that is not necessarily an accurate assumption.

An informal survey of members of Spiritual Directors International revealed that it is not unusual today for direction to take fewer than six sessions. While most directors see people over an extended time, as many as half of their spiritual direction relationships are short-term either in duration or in number of sessions. They may see people frequently over a brief period of time, or infrequently—as few as four or five times— over a period of years. This is not the intense, monthly, long-term relationship most contemporary directors are trained to expect. One colleague, after ten years of practicing the ministry of spiritual direction, wrote the following: "Most of my spiritual direction relationships last from two to five sessions. This has left me with some ambivalence and confusion, as my training . . . provided the model and the belief that spiritual direction relationships were long-term, slow, and quiet. . . . I have never shared this with another until your query came. But I'm aware I have had numerous questions as to whether this seemed to be others' experience or whether I had inadvertently ended up practicing a bogus variant of spiritual direction."

Other spiritual directors describe relationships that last a few sessions—or even just one session—and then resurface months or years later. "A few weeks ago, I received a letter from a woman I met with for less than an hour . . . ten years ago," another director wrote. "She wrote to tell me how important that time was for her. So—we never know how the Spirit may use us." Another colleague said she has begun to think of some of her work as "Christ kinship moments," single brief encounters that have an impact on the person's spiritual life. Such moments arise frequently when one is open to them.

These experiences are not recent developments rising out of our mobile, high-tech society. Rather, they have always been a norm for the practice of spiritual direction. During the era of the desert mothers and fathers, for example, pilgrims would endure days of rough travel for a single meeting or a few days with a gifted ascetic. Saint John Chrysostom provided direction to Olympias, a deaconess, in a series of four letters.[8] In the monastic community at Thavata, near Gaza, two famous directors provided care to hundreds of people by letter without ever seeing their directees face-to-face.[9] The Russian Orthodox Church has always recognized the *staretz*, a holy person who shapes lives across vast distances after a single meeting or a letter. Martin Luther and others provided brief spiritual direction in the form of infrequent letters to those seeking direction. In the medieval era, clergy and laity alike sought the advice of anchorites, holy men and women who provided wisdom to seekers, often without an ongoing pastoral relationship. In fact, it is likely that outside of monastic settings, most spiritual direction in history was brief in nature until the advent of modern psychology and its bias toward long-term therapy.

It is also a fact of parish life that most pastoral care is brief in nature; counseling by ministers, for example, typically happens in one to three sessions.[10] There is no reason to think that people seeking spiritual direction in a parish setting (or in another typical ministry setting, such as a hospital or nursing home chaplaincy) will necessarily want or expect long-term care when they seek spiritual direction. As many have argued, pastors are busy people with a number of widely disparate responsibilities. Learning to provide brief spiritual direction makes sense in today's parish. It allows two valuable resources—the pastor's time and the pastor's talents—to be made available to a greater number of people. Catholic spiritual director Adrian van Kaam warns against "regular, exclusive one-to-one" spiritual direction, saying, "It would be impossible to assure all people equally the availability of a regular personal spiritual director. To suggest such a utopia is to raise false expectations and subsequent frustrations."[11]

Thus, a better model of spiritual direction for the twenty-first century may be intermittent spiritual direction over a person's life span rather than ongoing, lifelong direction. This approach reflects the reality encountered by pastors and spiritual directors of our day. (Gone are the times when Kevin G. Culligan could recommend ten sessions to hear people's stories and evaluate whether they were fitting subjects for spiritual direction.)[12] The idea of intermittent spiritual direction over a person's life span is not new, however. Not only have we seen examples of this approach from ancient times, but in 1938 Hubert S. Box recommended that "occasional interviews at long intervals" were sufficient for most spiritual direction. And in 1989 Kenneth Leech wrote that "spiritual direction involves a number of temporary, though important, relationships during the course of one's life."[13]

DANGERS AND PITFALLS IN BRIEF SPIRITUAL DIRECTION

Brief spiritual direction is not a panacea, however. It has its own shortcomings as well as dangers and pitfalls to be avoided. Peter Verity, writing about single-session spiritual direction, warns that a short-term approach may lend itself to labeling or categorizing people's spiritualities in ways that are judgmental or that fail to take the directee's experience into full consideration.[14] I echo this concern. When I catch myself labeling or categorizing directees, I am aware that I have probably stepped from *not knowing* (as discussed in chapter 2) to *knowing* in ways that probably do not help the directee.

Verity also notes two other dangers relevant to short-term spiritual direction: a tendency for a director to oversimplify a directee's concerns and therefore offer easy answers, and an attempt to do too much in too little time, as if all of the directee's concerns or problems must be addressed before the spiritual direction relationship ends.[15]

Another pitfall, in my experience, is the insecurity and anxiety a pastor feels when a spiritual directee fails to return after one or two sessions. When brief spiritual direction is de facto rather than intentional, pastors tend toward three responses: blaming themselves for not providing what the directee was looking for, searching their experience for something that "went wrong" in the relationship, or attributing the end of the relationship to the directee's resistance—and thus pathologizing the person.

When spiritual direction relationships end earlier than expected, I take comfort in brief psychotherapy research that suggests most people who fail to return after one or two sessions do so because their initial concern has been relieved or because they gained sufficient resources to address their situation without further professional help. In spiritual direction, it is important to reflect on these "failed" relationships to identify ways in which the director might have alienated the directee. But when someone does not return for more sessions, perhaps it is also appropriate to celebrate rather than blame ourselves or pathologize the directee. Celebration grows from the assurance that God's presence in a brief spiritual direction relationship is sufficient to get directees "on track" spiritually and remind them of the resources already present in their lives (such as friends, Scripture, and a worshipping community) that can help them grow spiritually without ongoing spiritual direction.

CONCLUSION:
DEVELOPING AN INTENTIONALLY BRIEF APPROACH

There is no brevity in our ever-changing cradle-to-grave relationship with God. History and experience, however, do not reveal a need for a lifelong (or even long-term) relationship with a single spiritual director to survive the spiritual journey. Instead, assistance from a spiritual guide may be required at various crossroads along the way. Pastors and others offering spiritual counsel have much to gain from the underlying assumptions and even the methods of brief pastoral counseling. For their benefit, and for the benefit of those for whom they care, this book seeks to put spiritual direction into conversation with the theory and methods of brief pastoral counseling.

The following chapters establish a theological context for the practice of brief spiritual direction, explore the assumptions of brief pastoral counseling that inform brief spiritual direction, describe the tasks and structure of the first session of brief spiritual direction, introduce classic principles of Christian spiritual discernment, and describe and apply specific interventions appropriate to brief spiritual direction. The book concludes with chapters on brief spiritual direction for couples and families and a model for short-term group spiritual direction in the parish.

2

KNOWING UNKNOWING

Some pastors think they don't know enough or aren't "spiritual" enough to provide spiritual direction to others. "I can listen," they say, "but I don't know what else to do. And besides—I need some direction in my own spiritual life before I can start helping others!" But no matter how much pastors doubt their ability to provide spiritual direction, many discover that giving such guidance—through long-term, ongoing relationships or through occasional, brief encounters—is an important part of ministry in any setting.

So what can a hesitant or unprepared pastor do when someone asks for spiritual guidance? A first step is to acknowledge that what a spiritual director doesn't know can be as important as what she does know. After all, no one understands the ways of God at all times and places, and it is impossible for one person to know objectively how another "ought" to relate to God. It is true that some contemporary models of spiritual growth, such as James Fowler's "stages of faith,"[1] suggest that people progress through clear developmental stages in their lives with God. But these models cannot be used by a spiritual director to diagnose or prescribe the correct "next step" in someone's spiritual life. Simply put, no one's relationship with God fits neatly within precise developmental stages. Everyone is an exception.

This is a primary assumption of brief spiritual direction: everyone is an exception in one way or another to "normal" or "typical" spiritual development. Everyone is an exception because God acts in many different ways and people experience (and interpret) God's action and presence differently. What a spiritual director knows about God from his or her own training or experience may be less helpful to others than the director's ability to remain open and curious about two things: the ways in which the Holy One chooses to manifest in someone else's life at a particular time, and how that person goes about making sense of his or her experiences of God. This open and curious attitude is the heart of brief spiritual direction.

Adopting a stance of curiosity and openness, however, can be difficult for pastors and others with theological training who live and work in the dominant culture of North America. This culture values expertise and expert opinions, and seminary prepares pastors to serve as teaching elders, "experts" in religious knowledge. In addition, the people who surround pastors often want and expect them to be the resident experts on biblical interpretation, church history, human relationships, and spirituality. To resist the temptation to play the expert—and to stave off the expectation that being the expert is a role pastors ought to take on—contemporary spiritual directors may find it helpful to adopt the "not-knowing position" of brief pastoral counseling and secular psychotherapy.

The not-knowing position is a particular stance toward what it is possible to know—particularly what a person can and cannot know about someone else's experience. This stance carries a strong commitment to the ethical use of power in human relationships—a commitment that can strengthen the practice of spiritual direction by safeguarding against the authoritarian approaches to spiritual guidance that have sometimes dominated Christian tradition.

A working understanding of the not-knowing position and how spiritual directors can use it in their work can add significantly to the practice of brief spiritual direction. This chapter describes the not-knowing position and correlates it with Christian tradition by drawing first on an axiom of Dominican spirituality and then on a passage from Paul's letter to the church at Philippi. The not-knowing position can be easier to illustrate than to describe, however; for that reason, I will begin with a case example that contrasts a knowing position in spiritual direction with the not-knowing position I advocate.

THE NOT-KNOWING POSITION IN ACTION

Sharon knew she was called to ordained ministry, and her congregation and denomination affirmed it. Seminary was her next step, and it was more than possible: she was single, her children were grown, and she had the resources to pursue graduate theological education. But Henry, her aging parrot, kept her from enrolling.

Henry had been blinded by a previous owner, and he relied on Sharon for his care. She knew he would not be allowed in seminary housing, but she could not afford both tuition and a private apartment. Nor could she give Henry away; he was a one-person bird, and she was his person. He did not trust others and would accept food only from Sharon, who fed him by hand three times a day. She sometimes joked that owning Henry was like caring for a disabled spouse or aged parent. But she knew it was not funny that a commitment to a bird was keeping her from answering God's call. So late one night, she asked God in prayer to show her a solution to this dilemma.

The next morning, Sharon placed Henry's cage in a shady spot on her patio, as she usually did on warm spring mornings. While he whistled and muttered to the wild birds, Sharon went to take a shower. But when she returned to the patio, she found a snake in the process of eating Henry. It had slipped between the bars of the birdcage, and she watched in horror as it swallowed her pet. What was even more horrifying was that the snake—its belly now too fat to fit between the bars of the cage—could not escape.

Sharon was overwhelmed. Her dilemma was solved, but she wondered if her prayer had somehow caused the snake to attack Henry. Would God act with such violence to free someone to pursue a call to ministry? Sharon wrestled with her questions alone for several weeks. Then she decided to see a spiritual director.

This particular director, however, liked to play the expert. She dismissed Sharon's concerns about the connection between prayer and Henry's death. "God would never do anything like that," she said. "God acts in love to give life to creation. This event had nothing to do with your call to ministry." It was good theology, perhaps, but bad spiritual direction. Working from an expert, or knowing, position, the director assumed she understood something about God that Sharon needed to know. She imposed her own theology on Sharon's experience, attempting to correct Sharon's understanding so they would have a shared perception of God.

Luckily, Sharon did not give up on spiritual direction. Several days later, she saw a second spiritual director, who invited her to explore the events surrounding Henry's death by asking, "What would it be like to belong to a God who could act with such ferocity?" This director took a not-knowing position, assuming God might act in ways that were unfamiliar to him and to Sharon. Rather than responding to Sharon from his own knowledge and experience of God, or attempting to tell her what she "should" know about her experience, this director relied on Sharon's experience to inform his own understanding of the event and of how she made sense of it. He was aware that his knowledge was limited; to understand Sharon's subjective experience, he had to rely on her to tell him what it was like. As a result, he treated spiritual direction as a collaborative conversation rather than an opportunity to teach correct theology.

This approach to spiritual direction illustrates the essence of the not-knowing position.

DESCRIBING THE NOT-KNOWING POSITION

The concept of not-knowing first emerged in the literature of postmodern psychotherapy in the early 1990s. At that time, therapists, pastoral counselors, and other mental health professionals made passionate and persuasive arguments for the use of a non-expert, or "not-knowing," position in caring relationships. These arguments, which made practical and ethical claims about power and its place in helping relationships, grew from the conviction that people seeking care possess the expertise and knowledge necessary to reach their therapeutic goals. The idea of not knowing limits the helper's expertise to the therapeutic *relationship* and the *process* of therapy. Thus, a helping professional, such as a spiritual director, cannot claim "expert" or privileged knowledge of the *content* of another person's experiences, the meanings assigned to those experiences, or how others "should" or will address the difficulties they encounter. A therapist working from a not-knowing position, for example, would hesitate to diagnose someone as depressed and prescribe a particular treatment. Instead, that therapist would be more likely to accept the person's description of the problem as "feeling sad" and explore ways the person has discovered to keep sadness at bay.

While vast differences exist between spiritual direction and the counseling approaches in which the not-knowing position developed, I believe not knowing can shape spiritual direction relationships in important ways. First, assuming a stance of not knowing places boundaries on the spiritual director's expertise. Second, it can help the director avoid misusing power, which can happen almost unconsciously because of the emotional and spiritual vulnerability of the directee. Spiritual direction requires people to open their souls in an atypically intimate way; doing so requires tremendous risk and trust. The not-knowing position can protect a vulnerable directee from an overzealous or authoritarian director who asks questions or makes interpretations from a privileged or expert position. This in itself is a sufficient reason to seriously engage the not-knowing position in the process of brief spiritual direction.

Adopting a not-knowing position or stance, however, does not make the director powerless or suggest that the director knows nothing. Not knowing is different from knowing nothing, and directors should never withhold appropriate knowledge from directees. After all, spiritual directors bring to the conversation important understandings of Scripture, tradition, religious experience, and the ways of God—all of which are important to the process of spiritual direction. But the director's knowledge should not be the primary lens through which a directee's experiences are viewed. Meaning should not be imposed from (or by) the director's perspective.

Instead of imposing her own meaning on people's experiences, the spiritual director who works from a not-knowing position seeks to create an inviting space that allows true dialogue and collaboration to take place. Throughout the conversation, the director's actions and comments will reflect genuine openness and curiosity, a willingness to suspend her ways of knowing in order to see the world through the eyes of the directee. This requires a profound respect for the directee's competence and personal agency. It also requires the director to refuse to impose her own meanings or knowledge on directees. Any "knowledge" offered by the director is offered tentatively, as *one* way of viewing the situation rather than as *the* correct way of viewing.

For example, if a directee described a deep sadness in prayer that caused him to cry, a director working from a knowing position might say, "You are experiencing the 'prayer of tears.' That is a gift from God." A director working from a not-knowing position would offer the same knowledge more tentatively: "What you describe sounds similar to the 'prayer of tears.' I wonder if this experience is a gift God has offered to you." Likewise, if a directee described a sense of "coming home" in prayer, a director working from a knowing position might say, "Your feeling was a response to God's grace in your life; that sort of joyful 'homecoming' is a response to God." A director working from a not-knowing position would, again, offer the same knowledge more tentatively: "Did that joyful feeling seem like a response to God's presence in your life? Could it be related to grace?"

The not-knowing position, then, assumes that the director never completely understands what the directee is saying but is always "on the path" to understanding. Because the director's knowledge is held tentatively, her questions or comments during a spiritual direction conversation reflect "a genuine curiosity for that which is 'not-known' about that which has just been said."[2] This allows the directee's unique understandings of an experience—rather than the director's theory, technique, or interpretation—to dictate the content and movement of the spiritual direction conversation. Directees are free to accept or reject the "knowledge" offered by directors, depending on its fit with their own experiences and understandings.

A directee who refuses a director's knowledge or interpretations is not resistant or in denial, as much of spiritual direction literature suggests. Rather, rejection of the director's knowledge can indicate that the director has not yet fully understood the directee. Such rejection suggests the director needs to "know less," listening again to hear the directee's experiences and understandings with fresh ears rather than filtering information through the theological and psychological templates that shape the director's own understandings.

Listening in this manner, however, is difficult in a culture built on possessing and exercising expert knowledge. Not knowing can stretch a director by challenging her academic and practical knowledge as well as the pastoral identity and authority she has worked hard to develop. Not knowing is, in itself, a spiritual discipline; it requires a "deliberate immolation of the professional self," an immolation that keeps a director's understanding in a conversation from being "limited by prior experiences or theoretically formed truth, and knowledge."[3] The director listens in such a way that unheard or undervalued voices in a directee are granted the authority—the right to author one's own stories—that all beings created in the image of God deserve. As family therapist Harlene Anderson writes: "In my conversation with clients, . . . I do not want to deconstruct or instruct the marginal voice to make it what I know or think it should be. Instead, I want to create room for and learn about it. I want to immerse myself and be led into a client's world with an attitude and action that demonstrate sincere interest and respect, and that promote a client's feeling heard and confirmed."[4]

Not knowing is more than a psychotherapeutic technique. It is also theologically sound, and both Scripture and tradition offer compelling support for a not-knowing position in brief spiritual direction. This support includes the theological concept of the "darkness of God" (that part of God which is beyond human imagery and imagination) and the biblical concept of self-emptying described by the apostle Paul. These concepts provide pastors and other Christians with metaphors that help them understand and apply the not-knowing position in brief spiritual direction.

NICHOLAS OF CUSA AND "LEARNED IGNORANCE"

The idea that there are some things about God we cannot know is nothing new. The practice of eliminating what we do know about God until we are left with what we do not know—sometimes called the "negative way," or apophatic spirituality—is common to the writings of many

Christian mystics. In fact, the title of this chapter, "Knowing Unknowing," is a translation of a phrase found in the writings of Nicholas of Cusa, a fifteenth-century Dominican mystic.[5] Nicholas writes of "learned ignorance," the *docta ignorantia,* as a turning point in the human journey toward God. No matter how much we know or experience, Nicholas states, we cannot see or understand that which we most desire—the Holy One shrouded in divine darkness. Therefore, Nicholas says, "since the desire in us is not in vain, assuredly we desire to know that we do not know. If we can fully attain to this [knowledge of our ignorance], we will attain unto learned ignorance. For a man—even one very well versed in learning—will attain unto nothing more perfect than to be found to be most learned in the ignorance which is distinctively his. The more he knows that he is unknowing, the more learned he will be."[6]

In short, Nicholas urges us to discover how much we do not know about God rather than seeking to fill our ignorance with facts or experience. He wants us to savor our unknowing as part of the mystery of God—the divine darkness we can never completely know. For Nicholas, beginning to understand how much spiritual territory remains hidden to us, a dark forest never penetrated by the beam of our intellect or experience, tells us more about God than all of the theologies we could ever read or master. As Dominican scholar Richard Woods summarizes: "When we think we know what God is, we are furthest away from understanding. . . . It is only when we open both our minds and hearts to the Incomprehensible that we grow closer to God."[7]

In a similar way, we are often furthest from understanding another person when we think we know who or what that person is. Only by consistently seeking to uncover what is not known about people and their experiences of God—helping to give voice to that which has not yet been said or acknowledged—can we successfully guide others in their attempts to grow closer to God. In this way, the "knowing unknowing" of Nicholas intersects the not-knowing position of brief spiritual direction. A pastor providing brief spiritual direction attends to a directee in the same way Nicholas attends to the divine—by remembering that whatever we think we know about God cannot go unchallenged.

Likewise, whatever we think we know about another person's experiences of God cannot go unchallenged. We constantly seek the limits of our knowledge through an open and curious attitude. Being aware of our ignorance of God and others, and being willing to be taught about God by those others whose knowledge differs from our own in significant ways, is essential to providing spiritual direction in brief encounters. We empty ourselves of what we know in order to perceive God—to see flashes of the Divine, to feel God's pulse, to smell God's subtle fragrance, to hear the Holy One's still, small voice—in unexpected ways at unexpected places in the lives of others.

This is a task that requires deep humility and an acceptance of paradox. The paradox is that we have appropriate, general knowledge about life with God and about the process of spiritual direction, yet we do not know anything about a particular person's life with God or how spiritual direction might help that person. In brief spiritual direction, we use what we know appropriately to uncover what we do not yet know. This occurs through continually testing and challenging our understandings. "Whether in prayer, in thinking about God, in meditation, even in art, fixity of shape must never go unchallenged," writes Woods.[8] This practice of not knowing allows us to be open to the Holy Spirit. It also cleanses us of preconceived notions of who and what God might be so we can attend more closely to particular and often surprising manifestations of the Holy One in the experiences of those seeking spiritual guidance.

THE MIND OF CHRIST: NOT KNOWING AND SELF-EMPTYING

Perhaps the most compelling reason to adopt a not-knowing position in brief spiritual direction is that it reflects aspects of the mind of Christ as depicted in Scripture. In fact, the biblical letter to the church at Philippi includes an early liturgical hymn that might be understood as an example of "divine not knowing"—God setting aside divine power and knowledge in order to understand fully what it is to be human from a human point of view. The hymn is central to the letter the apostle Paul wrote when the Philippians needed encouragement in their life together. It illustrates one part of what "right relationship" means to Paul and for all Christians. Because spiritual direction is a type of relationship, it is helpful to explore this expression of right relationship that emerged from the early church, recorded and interpreted by Paul.

The passage, which scholars call the *kenosis* hymn, emphasizes the self-emptying nature of God. Paul introduces it by saying,

> If then there is any encouragement in Christ, any consolation from love, any sharing in the Spirit, any compassion and sympathy, make my joy complete: *be of the same mind*, having the same love, being in full accord and of one mind. Do nothing from selfish ambition or conceit, but in humility regard others as better than yourselves. Let each of you look not to your own interests, but to the interests of others. Let *the same mind* be in you that was in Christ Jesus. (Phil. 2:1-5, emphasis added)

He then describes the mind of Christ by saying that Jesus,

> though he was in the form of God,
>> did not regard equality with God
>> as something to be exploited,
> but *emptied himself,*
>> taking the form of a slave,
>> being born in human likeness.
> And being found in human form,
>> he humbled himself
>> and became obedient to the point of death—
>> even death on a cross. (Phil. 2:6-8, emphasis added)

Two aspects of this passage seem important to the practice of spiritual direction from a not-knowing position: the notion of Christ "emptying himself" and the idea that humans should "be of the same mind" as this self-emptying Christ.

The Greek word for "emptied" in this passage is transliterated *kenosis* (hence the scholarly designation of the passage as the *kenosis* hymn). The word has a unique use in the letter to the Philippians, where it carries a sense of being "poured out" for others. This *kenotic,* or self-emptying, metaphor has been important to pastoral caregivers for centuries. Contemporary pastoral theologian Donald Capps calls proclamation through pastoral care "an act of kenosis, of assuming the burden of another person's problems and abandoning oneself with the act of 'being with' vulnerable, suffering, and distressed persons."[9] I affirm the ministry of presence that Capps describes, but I think he has settled for a limited and less than exegetically satisfying understanding of *kenosis* and its place in pastoral care and spiritual direction.

While a detailed exegesis of the passage is beyond the scope of this chapter, I want to summarize some ways in which Christians traditionally have understood Christ's self-emptying. Then I want to argue that one recent understanding of self-emptying correlates well with the not-knowing position—especially because the scriptural passage from which we draw the concept of Christ's self-emptying illustrates not just the nature of God but also how those who are in Christ should live: with humble vulnerability toward God and others in community.

This emphasis on the passage's didactic nature is a recent development in scriptural studies. For much of Christian history, theologians related self-emptying only to the nature of God. Specifically, they believed it related to the interplay of Jesus' human and divine natures. This interpretation rises in part from the *kenosis* hymn's statement that

Jesus, as a human being, did not regard equality with God as something to be exploited or "grasped after" (to use the translation of the New International Version), as Adam and Eve "grasped" for divine knowledge of good and evil. Theologians in this tradition advanced two primary understandings of Christic self-emptying. The first speaks of Jesus "temporarily *relinquishing* divine powers," while the second speaks of Jesus as "*pretending* to relinquish divine powers whilst actually retaining them."[10]

Historically, theologians drew on these interpretations to support the status quo in the power dynamics of the church and society. These interpretations were used, first, to support the idea that God does not suffer—that is, that Christ humbly emptied himself of divine power prior to the crucifixion, suffering only in his human form. Second, they were used to argue that imitating Christ requires humble acceptance of what comes to us (much as the passive laity accepts the "expert" understanding of the clergy, or as the suffering poor accept the domination of the upper classes, or as a psychotherapy client accepts the yoke of "expert care" in classic psychoanalysis).

More recently, however, British theologian Sarah Coakley has identified several other understandings of Christ's self-emptying. Two are important to our current purpose. One imagines self-emptying as Jesus "choosing *never to have* certain (false and worldly) forms of power." The other sees self-emptying as "*revealing* 'divine power' to be intrinsically 'humble' rather than 'grasping.'"[11] From these perspectives, self-emptying is a choice about power in relationships; it becomes a "*special* form of power-in-vulnerability"[12]—power viewed not as a "blueprint for a perfect human moral response [that is, requiring humble acceptance of what comes to us], but as revelatory of the 'humility' of the *divine* nature."[13] From this perspective, divine humility can be seen in God's refusal to assume an understanding of what it is to be human, instead, letting go of—pouring out—divine power and knowledge, emptying the Holy Self, in order to experience human being as humans experience it.

For Coakley, Christ's self-emptying reveals that divine power is a "paradox of power and vulnerability."[14] For human beings, that paradox always carries the temptation to use power in ways that suit our own needs or that make ourselves look good but are abusive to other people. "If 'abusive' human power is thus always potentially within our grasp," Coakley asks, "how can we best approach the healing resources of a non-abusive divine power? How can we hope to invite and channel it, if not by a patient opening of the self to its transformation?"[15] She concludes that "we can only be 'empowered' . . . if we cease to set the agenda, if we 'make space' for God to be God."[16] This is similar to a caregiver who has adopted the not-knowing position, intentionally deciding not to set the agenda for a caring conversation but making space for the person seeking care to set that agenda. For human beings to imitate the self-emptying of Christ, then, requires "an ascetical commitment of some subtlety, a regular and willed *practice* of ceding and responding to the divine."[17]

Here is where self-emptying and not knowing come together. As Christ emptied himself of certain types of (potentially abusive) power in order to experience life as a created being—to see and experience life from our perspective, even suffering death as we do—so also the spiritual director turns away from preconceived, expert knowledge in order to see and experience God from the directee's perspective. Thus, in the words of Harlene Anderson, the not-knowing position is related "to what I do with what I know or think I know. . . . Preferences and opinions . . . do not come from a position of privileged knowing. . . . What I am preoccupied by or value is submitted with humility, tentativeness, and openness to alternatives."[18] The director risks two things in this process: being wrong and learning something new about God.[19] Adopting a self-emptying, not-knowing stance requires a director to question his or her present assumptions about God and God's relationships to human beings.

Maintaining this not-knowing or self-emptying position can be difficult for creatures trapped in sin. Often, we want to grasp after what we know (or think we know) as if it were an absolute truth—not recognizing that grasping after knowledge in this way risks idolatry. A self-emptying, not-knowing approach to brief spiritual direction, then, requires us to turn in humility to God with a contemplative attitude. Those seeking to foster a practice of brief spiritual direction that takes seriously the paradox of divine power and vulnerability choose to allow directees to teach us what they know about God from their own experiences while listening contemplatively for the stirring of Spirit within the conversation. To succeed at this, we strive to empty ourselves of our selves, our knowledge, and our experiences in order to make room for what we do not know about God.

This attitude of not knowing gains further support from another phrase in Paul's *kenosis* passage—that of "having the same mind" as Christ. The verb that Paul uses here to speak of having the same mind is related to the Greek philosophical concept of *phronesis*, or practical wisdom. Practical wisdom involves action based on an inner attitude, an attitude learned through experience rather than rooted in theoretical or technical knowledge. This attitude practices letting go, surrendering the self and giving up a concern for outcome in order to be present to the

Other (who is both divine and human) and to obey God for the sake of the Other. The linear, logical thinking of the rational mind is replaced by a "heart" knowledge, which is founded both in a surrender to the reality experienced by others and in a lived awareness of the presence of God. This intuitive knowledge of the heart (in which the heart is understood as an organ that perceives divine realities) dictates who and how the director needs to be in relation to the directee and what sort of spiritual guidance is necessary in a given situation.[20] To approach life in this way might be one way of "having the same mind" as Christ.

It is important to note that for the apostle Paul, Christ is wisdom personified: the living, breathing presence of practical wisdom. The mind of Christ is a mind that empties itself of what it was before or what it possessed before—including theoretical and technical knowledge of humanity, the knowledge only the creator can have of the created—in order to be fully responsive and obedient to God in a new context and as a new sort of being. This is the pattern for what humans are meant to be. In promoting the idea that Christians should have this same mind, Paul seems to advocate human action born of a particular attitude—a "knowing how" rather than a "knowing that" or a "knowing what." The wisdom of the mind of Christ is a self-emptying, not-knowing wisdom. As much as possible, this is the mind with which a spiritual director approaches a spiritual direction conversation—especially in the practice of brief spiritual direction, in which long-term relationships with directees and future opportunities to correct mistakes born of grasping after our own wisdom might be limited.

CONCLUSION:
LETTING GO OF POWER TO BE GRASPED BY GOD

If, then, we take seriously the self-emptying wisdom of the Christian mind—a self-emptying illustrated by Nicholas of Cusa's concept of knowing unknowing—the practice of brief spiritual direction becomes a process of suspending what we think we know in order to understand fully the experiences of the directee. Then, listening to God through the heart, the practitioner of brief spiritual direction turns to *appropriate knowing*[21] to evaluate what the directee has said about God against what is known about God through Scripture, tradition, experience, and reason. The person practicing brief spiritual direction is always ready to accept that the directee might know something about God that the director does not.

In my experience, this sort of practice is easy to speak of but difficult to do. Many pastors who want to practice spiritual direction grasp after their seminary expertise, their knowledge of exegesis, history, and theology, to control the process of direction or to offer "content" responses that miss the heart of the other person and the heart of God's call to both director and directee. This sort of grasping after our own knowledge can set up a subtle power differential in which the pastor may struggle to maintain a superior position on the basis of specialized training.

Spiritual directors committed to the practice of not knowing, however, seek to empty themselves of claimed expertise about the experiences of directees in order to be obedient to the leading of the Spirit—to discern through the heart how the Holy One is shaping the person, how the person might be distorting that process, and how the director might fruitfully enter the conversation already occurring between God and the directee. Doing this well demands the mind of Christ, who emptied himself of power to enter human reality with vulnerability and then was obedient to what the situation demanded. Serving as a spiritual director asks us to make not knowing a spiritual discipline, a practice of seeking to have the same mind, the same humility, the same power in vulnerability as the Christ of the Gospel narratives.

3

GUIDANCE FROM
BRIEF PASTORAL COUNSELING

Jill was an occasional visitor to our Sunday worship, and although we enjoyed friendly banter as she left the sanctuary, she had never been open to my phone calls or suggestions that we get together to visit. Now, nearly a year after first worshipping with the congregation, she called the office to ask if I was familiar with spiritual direction. I said I had several, ongoing direction relationships with people in the community. Her reply was adamant: "I'm not looking for a lifelong spiritual director," she said. "I just need to check in about my prayer life once and maybe get some suggestions for paying better attention to my relationship with God. Can you handle that?"

I suggested we meet for a conversation and make a plan from there. A week later, after an hour-long meeting, Jill agreed to call when she needed a second appointment. That was more than a year ago. She still drops in for worship every other month or so, telling me each time how grateful she is for our long-ago conversation. She says it clarified her relationship with God. She hasn't asked for additional guidance since our session.

Most communities harbor many people like Jill. Some are active in congregations; many are not. How does a pastor know which of these people are likely candidates for brief spiritual direction? Perhaps the easiest way to find out is to ask. The questions "How many times do you expect to meet for spiritual direction?" and "How many weeks or months or years do you think we'll continue meeting?" can quickly identify a person seeking brief spiritual direction. A short-term stance is most appropriate with people like Jill, who expect fewer than five spiritual direction sessions in a year. Likewise, a person who hesitates to commit to a spiritual direction relationship (also like Jill) might benefit from a short-term orientation. It is not unusual for such directees to meet with a director only once.

Of course, you should not rely on only the person seeking direction to determine if a spiritual direction relationship should be brief. Your own situation may also suggest a brief approach. If you doubt your ongoing availability (because you are moving away, for example, or expecting a child) or if you know circumstances will limit your future interactions with a person (for instance, if you meet a potential directee during an out-of-town conference or while traveling), you should almost always adopt a brief stance.

In such instances, it can help for the director and directee to borrow a technique from brief pastoral counseling: making a covenant to meet for a certain number of sessions and then to review whether the relationship should continue. I typically covenant with brief directees to meet three to five times, reviewing our process and progress during the final meeting. That way we can make a deliberate decision about whether to continue our spiritual direction relationship. If we decide the relationship should end, we spend the final session reviewing the growth that occurred (or did not occur!) for the directee, naming the spiritual themes or metaphors that informed the process, taking time for both of us to speak from the heart about what the relationship has meant to us and our journeys, and giving thanks together in prayer for the relationship and for God's presence in it. I often ask the directee to say the closing prayer.

Those who practice short-term spiritual direction will find it helpful to be familiar with the assumptions and practices of brief pastoral counseling. Many approaches to brief therapy exist, but I find the collaborative approaches developed in the past fifteen years (including narrative, solution-focused, and competency-based models) particularly helpful.[1] Several of these approaches have been adapted for pastoral care and counseling, and all of them share a theoretical base in social constructionism—the idea that we form our hopes, problems, beliefs, relationships, and the meanings we give to our experiences out of our interactions with others.[2]

These therapies share a number of assumptions about people, about the nature of helping relationships, and about the process of caring for others. This chapter outlines eight common assumptions of these models, correlating them with Christian spiritual theology. (Spiritual theology is the traditional name for the base of "theory" for the ministry of spiritual direction.) A short case example at the close of the chapter shows how these two theoretical bases—spiritual theology and brief pastoral counseling—can inform a pastor's interventions during brief spiritual direction.

KEY ASSUMPTIONS OF BRIEF PASTORAL COUNSELING

Eight key assumptions of brief pastoral counseling lend themselves to the practice of brief spiritual direction. While it might be tempting for readers to scan this information (or to skip it altogether) because of its "theoretical" nature, I encourage a close reading. The ideas presented here challenge some foundational assumptions of North American culture. They are also quite different from the psychological ideas that influence the dominant culture and shape the ways in which the industrialized West approaches caregiving. Although these assumptions are at odds with popular culture (just as the gospel is often also at odds with popular culture), they generally fit well with some Christian wisdom about human beings and about the ways God relates to the created order.[3]

Overall, these models of brief pastoral counseling seek to do the following.

Avoid diagnostic labels and pathologies. Brief pastoral counseling assumes that the problem, not the person, is the problem. That means a problem or difficulty faced by a parishioner is not seen as a personal fault or weakness located within the individual, but is viewed as something oppressing the person from outside. A spiritual director working from this assumption seeks to free people from those things that keep them separate from God. For example, imagine that a directee says, "I'm too depressed to pray." Rather than saying, "What's going on inside that keeps you from praying?" a director working from a brief perspective might respond, "How does the depression keep you from praying? Are there times you can stand up to or 'pray through' the depression?" The difference is subtle but important.

This commitment to avoiding diagnostic labels and pathologies is consistent with classical spiritual direction. The desert mothers and fathers who pioneered Christian spiritual guidance were less likely to label a person as "lazy" or "distracted in prayer" than to explore how a negative spirit was distracting the person from God or convincing the person to spend time in activities other than prayer. Beneath this assumption is a conviction that God empowers people to stand up to those things that turn them away from Spirit. God is at work to set people free from those things that oppress them.

This perspective also assumes that human nature is basically good. We are naturally oriented toward God and made in the image and likeness of God, but powers and situations at work in the world thwart our natural tendencies. Sinfulness is understood less as a problem of will or as an inner state than as a temptation or net that snares people from outside. Deadly thoughts and behaviors attack us, luring us away from our original nature as the image of God.

Emphasize people's existing strengths and resources. Brief pastoral counselors working from collaborative models assume that all people, no matter how problematic their lives, have strengths and abilities that can contribute to improving things. Much time in counseling is devoted to identifying and building on these strengths. People's strengths and resources may include attitudes, material resources, ways of coping, previous experiences of success, and various relationships, including relationships with God.

The assumption that people are naturally gifted with strengths and resources rejects our culture's tendency to focus on weaknesses or to fixate on problems and ignore what is going well. Instead, the brief pastoral counselor sees legitimate needs and tendencies as opportunities that open a person to a sense of multiple possibilities, that give hope to improve life in ways that reflect the person's own preferences, and that build on the gifts God has given the person. A spiritual director working from this assumption might say, "You've told me all the reasons why discursive prayer doesn't work for you. Tell me about the gifts you have for prayer—the unique ways in which you communicate with God or become aware of God's activity in your life."

While this approach needs to be tempered by an awareness of sin and evil within individual people and in cultural or social systems, emphasizing strengths, gifts, resources, and abilities is wholly consistent with classical spiritual direction. William J. Connolly, a pillar of Jesuit spiritual direction in the United States, has written that "there is an approach to 'direction' that concentrates primarily on a person's strengths and another that concentrates primarily on [the person's] weaknesses, and the choice between these approaches is a crucial one."[4] A focus on a person's strengths further reflects the theological stance that human nature is basically good and that God is at work in creation to achieve the divine purposes revealed by the incarnation of Jesus Christ.

Find exceptions to the difficulties people face. Exceptions, or times when difficulties are absent or less troubling, always exist. The trick is to identify those exceptions, make sure they are significant to the person seeking care, and then amplify and expand the exceptions to establish a foundation for a new experience of life free of (or less influenced by) a particular problem or difficulty. From this perspective, change is inescapable and always brings a chance to make life better. Problems or difficulties are temporary; they exist only because of the power we give them by naming them (and focusing on them) as problems. The brief pastoral counselor assumes God is always working to make life more abundant for all people; the task of the caregiver and care receiver is to collaborate with what God is doing to make a particular difficulty a thing of the past.

In some ways, this assumption reflects Brother Lawrence's "practice of the presence of God." From this perspective, God is always present in our lives; the reality of the gospel is as near as our next breath. We must train ourselves, however, to be aware of God's presence. The idea that God supports and sustains all of creation—that creation could not exist if God were not always at work repairing the torn strands of the web of being—is the ground of spiritual theology. This premise forms the context of the practice of spiritual direction: God is always at work in our lives in ways we do not realize, and we can become more aware of God's call if we reflect on God's activity in our lives with the intention of discerning an appropriate response. Identifying and building on exceptions to our difficulties is one way of identifying and responding to God's presence in our lives.

People seeking spiritual direction often complain that God feels distant or absent. It is important to affirm and explore a directee's sense of abandonment by God. But a spiritual director who takes seriously the assumption that there are always exceptions to our experiences of problems or difficulties will also prompt the directee to look for recent times when God has been near or present. "Tell me when God has felt less distant," the director might say. "Has there ever been a time when God has only been 70 or 80 percent absent, rather than 100 percent?" Identifying these exceptions in the directee's experience of God can become a foundation for new experiences of the presence and activity of God. These experiences have always existed, but they were previously overlooked because of a blanket assumption that God had abandoned or moved away from the directee. It is true that God sometimes does "move away" from people; the ways in which God's presence has become familiar to them are no longer fruitful. Identifying the times and places where God is a little nearer may indicate a call to a new direction or a new way of relating to and experiencing God.

Establish clear and specific goals. Only by understanding what change is desired and how they will know the change has occurred can people make good use of brief pastoral counseling. Without a clear goal, the purpose of the conversation between a pastor and a parishioner will be uncertain, and neither person may know when a final destination has been reached. Likewise, the brief spiritual director must understand why people initiate spiritual direction and what results they hope to see or what benefits they hope to attain. Without a clear picture of the directee's goals or intentions for spiritual direction, the director cannot be certain what paths might contribute to the journey of spiritual direction.

A goal orientation is nothing new for spiritual direction. This ministry has always been a teleological, or goal-oriented, activity. Typically, two goals predominate in spiritual direction: (1) identifying God's activity in a person's life and (2) discerning an appropriate response. Spiritual theology includes a third, broader goal, which has various names in the tradition: union with Christ, participation in the life of God, the beatific vision, *theosis* or transformation into the likeness of God. Classical spiritual direction understood direction as an aid to sanctification, the gradual and active transformation of a broken, sinful person into someone holy. Spiritual direction seeks to remove from the directee's life anything blocking this transformation or preventing a fuller experience of union with God in daily activities.

Brief spiritual direction keeps all three of these traditional goals in mind: identifying God's presence and action, discerning an appropriate response, and moving toward union with God in daily life. But the brief spiritual director also attends to the directee's more immediate goals or reasons for seeking spiritual direction. "You want to be closer to God," a director might say, "and spiritual direction is a good way to pursue that goal. But how will you know when you are closer to God? What will be different about your thoughts, feelings, and actions when you and God are closer to each other?" A directee's answers to these questions can narrow the focus of spiritual direction, helping the director pinpoint the experiences a directee finds significant rather than working toward the vague goal of "being closer to God."

Negotiate rather than impose goals and solutions. In brief pastoral counseling, the pastor and the person seeking help "co-create" a new reality. As discussed in chapter 2, they share power in a mutual, collaborative relationship that respects the self-determinacy of the person seeking help. This means pastors try to avoid assuming they know the goal of counseling or *the* solution to an individual's difficulty. Rather, they negotiate goals and solutions together with the person seeking care.

Behind this assumption is an expectation that human relationships should be mutual and empowering, based on consensus rather than on an imbalance of power. Brief pastoral counseling emphasizes that people need to feel heard and validated and that the process of receiving care needs to enhance people's sense of self-agency rather than emphasizing a submissive attitude or coercing them into particular ways of responding or relating to God.

This assumption may conflict with ancient models of spiritual direction, which tended to demand absolute obedience from directees. (Contemporary approaches to spiritual direction are much less authoritarian.) The desert mothers and fathers expected directees to submit themselves to the director's authority at all times; their direction relationships featured a shared respect between director and directee but assumed the director always knew what was best for the directee. The spiritual director was understood to be shaping the directee toward a greater goal than the directee might perceive or understand. Thus, the assumption of brief pastoral counseling that goals and solutions should be negotiated between the pastor and the parishioner, with each person contributing unique resources to the process, may conflict with classical spiritual direction.

Directees in brief spiritual direction risk idolatry of the self if they do not grant some authority to the director, but the director needs to be careful in claiming and exercising that authority. As emphasized in chapter 2, the skilled brief spiritual director practices both *not knowing* and *appropriate knowing*. If a directee insists that she does not want to make a commitment to a congregation or spiritual community, for example, a practitioner of brief spiritual direction might say, "I know your goal is to focus on your individual relationship with God, and that you do not feel that a community of believers would add to your experience of God right now. Maybe you are correct; certainly, I want to respect your sense of what God is calling you to right now. But I hope you are not making an idol of your individual relationship to God. Being in community is not just an important or optional part of Christian spirituality. It is essential to Christian spirituality, and it is a consistent emphasis of the spiritual paths of many religious traditions throughout history. I believe God is calling you to community in important ways if you will listen with an openness to hearing that call."

Focus on the present and future. In brief pastoral counseling, the past is of secondary importance to the present and future. Pastors working from a brief counseling model do not assume, as do many psychological approaches, that past experiences create the difficulties people face in the present. Rather, pastors working from a brief model believe placing too much emphasis on the past can impede growth and change. Looking to the future is the key to nurturing hope for a different life.

Likewise, Christian spiritual theology affirms that the present is the best guide to understanding how God is active in a person's life and what ways God is calling the person to be faithful to the future promised in

Christ. Spiritual theology has placed less emphasis on the eschatological (or ultimate) goal of the Christian journey than on the present. (This may be one reason the future receives less emphasis in classical spiritual direction than in the theory of brief pastoral counseling.) However, in brief spiritual direction, an emphasis on the present and future keeps directees focused on an appropriate response to God's action in their lives *now*. This focus is consistent with the emphasis of the desert mothers and fathers, who used everyday, common activities—eating and sleeping, working and playing—as the starting point for spiritual direction conversations.

Thus, a director adopting a brief orientation might listen carefully to a directee's stories of past experiences. (In fact, reliving, rehashing, and mourning the loss of spiritual high points—so-called "mountaintop experiences"—is a common focus among directees, especially early in the spiritual direction process.) But the brief spiritual director will always return the conversation to the present by saying, for example, "I know those experiences were important to you. But how have you experienced God's presence in the last week? The last day? How do you hope your relationship with God changes in the future? In what ways is God calling you to more abundant life, a life lived in the New Jerusalem promised in the New Testament?" (Once the brief spiritual director has listened to the directee reflect on these questions, it is important to seek exceptions: "How are you already experiencing even a little bit of that abundant life? In what small ways is the New Jerusalem already a reality in your life?")

Affirm small changes as a means to bigger changes. A small change in one part of life can often trigger a bigger change in other areas. For example, a mother who stops clenching her teeth as she struggles to dress her toddler may find that both she and her child adopt a less combative attitude toward other daily tasks. Brief pastoral counseling uses this dynamic to help people identify tiny, achievable actions that can send ripples through their lives. In this way, people who find a major life change too daunting to attempt can achieve tremendous positive growth one tiny, nonthreatening step at a time.

Likewise, classical spiritual direction has affirmed that small steps on the spiritual journey have broader impacts and can carry us through strenuous and demanding territory. Spending fifteen minutes in silence each day focused on the love of God can create a reservoir of peaceful quiet that a person can tap into during anxious or hectic times. Adding a humility-based bow to the end of a prayer (or during the phrase "thy will be done" in the Lord's Prayer) can make a person more receptive to (and less rebellious toward) the sovereignty of God in her life. God responds to each small move we make toward the Divine, adding the power of the Holy Spirit's energy to the tiny amount of energy we expend. Spiritual direction attends to the gradual *process* of being transformed in Christ's image. It does not attempt the transformation overnight.

Tailor care to the individual. Brief pastoral counseling is not a one-size-fits-all, cookie-cutter approach. Because people are the experts about their own lives, brief pastoral counseling pays close attention to the needs and meanings of the person seeking care, shaping the counseling process to that person's particular circumstances. This approach respects the diversity of human beings.

Similarly, brief spiritual direction recognizes there is no "protocol" or universal process that serves all directees equally well. Although we are all one in Christ, great diversity is built into our unity, as reflected in the Christian doctrine of the Trinity. Thus, the pastor must listen closely to the directee, adjusting questions and interventions to accommodate the particularities of the directee and the directee's unique relationship with God. This practice reflects the conviction in spiritual theology that the Holy Spirit, not the human director, is the true director. The process of spiritual direction is shaped by the Spirit in ways unique to each directee. The director who forgets this has violated a basic assumption of the practice of Christian spiritual direction.

ANNA'S DILEMMA: A BRIEF SPIRITUAL DIRECTION RESPONSE

For three years, Rev. Gail Kohl has served as the only pastor in a tiny rural community on the Great Plains. Although drawn to the area by its natural beauty, the long history of the congregation, and the honesty and deep faith of the people who live in and around town, Gail still feels like an outsider most of the time. Two ways she copes with her isolation as a single, female pastor are by making an annual retreat to a monastery in the nearby mountains and by meeting quarterly with her own spiritual director. Gail's value to the church and community has been affirmed recently as she has begun receiving more and more requests for individual and family counseling. This new emphasis in her ministry has caused Gail to start reading books and watching video-tapes about brief approaches to pastoral counseling.

One of Gail's church members is Anna, a thirty-year-old mother of two who lives on a ranch outside of town. Anna grew up in Rev. Gail's church, which was founded by her great-grandparents. Anna left town for four years to attend college in the state capital; after graduation she returned to the area, married her college sweetheart, and devoted her business acumen and accounting degree to her family's cattle-raising business. She remains deeply involved in the church, playing the piano during worship and serving on the fellowship committee. Her husband, Dale, although new to the church, was recently elected an elder. Anna and Dale's older son is four years old; the younger is two.

Two months ago, Anna approached Gail after church, asking if she had time to talk. Over a cup of coffee, Anna revealed that she felt torn between her love for God and her love for her family. Praying about the dilemma, she said, felt "empty and hollow," like the sound of the winter wind blowing through the hills on the ranch. She wanted to spend more time alone with God, hiking and praying, and resented her husband and sons for drawing her attention away from God. Anna asked Gail to help her figure out how God wanted her to balance her time and affections. Gail interpreted this request for help in listening to God as an issue to be addressed through spiritual direction rather than through counseling. But she wanted her recent learning in brief pastoral counseling to shape her spiritual direction response to Anna's dilemma.

At the initial meeting, the pair agreed to meet three more times to listen for God's response to Anna's dilemma. Gail mostly listened during the first conversation over coffee, allowing Anna to reveal her feelings and talk about the ways in which her dilemma affected her daily life. In their second meeting, Gail gently probed to help clarify Anna's goal for spiritual direction, something she did because of her reading in brief pastoral counseling. They agreed that Anna wanted to "feel more joy in loving both God and family" rather than feeling torn between the two. More specifically, Anna said she hoped God would show her how to love God at the same time that she was spending time with her family. She would know this had happened, she said, when "loving God and loving my three boys—Dale and our sons—happens all at the same time."

In their third meeting, Gail asked Anna what God had shown her since they had last talked, two weeks earlier.

> Anna: I don't know, Gail. I really don't. When I'm spending time alone with God, prayer seems wonderful. I feel really connected to Jesus, and the dilemma with my boys doesn't seem so important. But when I'm back at home, feeding the cows or washing dishes or trying to keep up with laundry, I feel so distracted from God. I start to feel angry at my three boys all over again.
>
> Gail: That sounds so frustrating! (*Anna nods.*) I know you said whenever you're home you feel totally distracted

from God. (*Anna nods again.*) Has there ever been a time in the past two weeks when you've been with Dale and the boys like you usually are but you've felt less distracted from God? (*Gail seeks an exception, focusing on Anna's recent experience and the "stuff" of daily life.*)

Anna: You mean a time when I sort of knew God was there even though I was with my family? (*Now it's Gail's turn to nod.*) Hmm. I don't think so. But maybe— maybe at breakfast the other morning. Dale was laughing with the boys, and I was sitting there drinking a cup of coffee and thinking how much I loved them, and I felt the same peace for a minute that I feel when I'm praying alone.

Gail: That sounds wonderful! How were you able to be aware of God at that moment? (*Gail focuses on Anna's gift of being aware of God's presence and affirms the assumption that God is always present and active in Anna's life.*)

Anna: I don't think I was aware of God! I just felt that peace. But maybe I also said a little prayer, just a "thank you," just before that peaceful feeling came.

Gail: The peace came after you prayed. (*Anna nods.*) And you prayed right in the middle of breakfast, with a dirty skillet right there on the stove and a hot coffee cup in your hands? Not all alone up in the hills or at church? That's amazing! (*Anna laughs.*) How was God there for you at that moment? (*Gail directs Anna's attention to God's presence and action in her life.*)

Anna: Well . . . maybe God prompted the prayer—maybe when I felt how much I loved my boys, God sort of tapped me on the shoulder to say, "They're my gift to you." And then I just said that prayer without thinking about it. I didn't even say it, really—I just felt it in my soul. (*Pause.*) That's funny—I almost always pray out loud, not in my head. (*Anna notices a small change in her prayer life that might lead to larger changes.*)

Gail: That seems like an important shift to notice. But I also want to ask—does God often "tap you on the shoulder" and remind you that your boys are God's gift?

Anna: God probably does it all the time—I just never notice! (*They laugh.*) Maybe I should pay more attention.

> Gail: It seems important to me that you did more than pay attention—you also responded with a spontaneous prayer.
>
> Anna: Yes. That does seem important, doesn't it?
>
> Gail: Could we maybe take a few minutes in silence right now to listen to what God might be saying—to see if God taps you on the shoulder again? I'm wondering if you will hear something about how to respond to this change in your typical prayer habits. (*Gail shifts the conversation to discerning an appropriate response to God's presence and action in Anna's life.*)

This case example illustrates how some assumptions of brief pastoral counseling work in tandem with basic tenets of spiritual theology to shape the process of brief spiritual direction. First, in an early session, Gail helped Anna identify an immediate goal that would help her make progress on the path of sanctification toward the ultimate goal of union with God. Second, Gail's conviction that God is present and active in Anna's life at all moments led her to seek exceptions to Anna's experience of her family "always" making her feel distant from God. Third, Gail did not locate the source of the difficulty in prayer as being "inside" Anna, nor did she label Anna as depressed, codependent, or resistant to God. Rather, she treated Gail as someone who had gifts and skills for relating to God and worked to uncover those strengths. Fourth, Gail gently directed Anna to focus on the present, and on everyday experiences, rather than on her past, or "mountaintop," experiences with God. Fifth, Gail assumed change was taking place in the way Anna communicates with God and pursued that change when Anna affirmed the assumption by speaking about a new type of prayer experience. Sixth, Gail used the same simple, everyday language and metaphor that Anna used rather than using "churchy" or theological language—reflecting her assumptions both that Anna was the expert on her own experience and that Gail's care should be adapted to Anna's unique experience and ways of communicating.

The conversation between Gail and Anna demonstrates how the assumptions of brief pastoral counseling work with the tenets of spiritual theology to inform brief spiritual direction. But how does a pastor approach the first—and sometimes *only*—session of brief spiritual direction? The next chapter addresses this important stage in the practice of brief spiritual direction.

4

THE FIRST SESSION

Deacon Juan Gonzalez watched from the window as Wendy Grey pulled into the church parking lot. On Sunday Juan had taught about praying with Scripture, and afterward Wendy asked to meet with him; she wanted to talk about her prayer life. Flattered by her request, Juan quickly said yes. But now his fingers tapped nervously on the windowsill. "What have I gotten myself into?" he thought. "I don't know how to talk to someone about her prayer life!" As Wendy knocked on the office door, he offered a silent prayer: "God, help me get through this without messing up too badly!"

Juan's anxiety is not unusual; many spiritual directors suffer from the first-meeting jitters each time they begin a new guidance relationship. Research suggests many pastoral caregivers are introverts; meeting new people and establishing new relationships can be uncomfortable for them, and even extroverted pastors find that relationships become easier the longer they last. The first meeting with a new directee, then, can cause anxiety for any spiritual director. This may be particularly true if the director suspects the relationship will be brief. In short-term spiritual direction, there simply is not enough time to establish the deep-rooted relationships many pastors value.

This chapter seeks to relieve the anxiety associated with first meetings by helping pastors make the most of the first (and sometimes only) session with a person seeking spiritual direction. The following topics are addressed:

- deciding whether brief spiritual direction is a good fit with a particular directee
- determining the structure and flow of a first session of brief spiritual direction
- hearing the directee's initial story
- setting goals for the direction relationship
- understanding typical concerns raised in a first meeting
- establishing a covenant of care between the director and the directee.

The stages of the first session, and the tasks for each, are outlined in figure 1 (see page 40). These stages and tasks are offered as a general guideline, not an ironclad and immutable process. To some extent, the stages and tasks described can be mixed, matched, and interwoven in a variety of ways to best serve the unique relationship between a particular director and a particular directee. The relationship, not the process, should be primary, and it is important for the director to establish a relaxed, reverent, and contemplative tone from the beginning.

WHEN TO PRACTICE SHORT-TERM SPIRITUAL DIRECTION

The first step in providing spiritual direction, short- or long-term, is to clarify the sort of help the person expects from you. Pastors should not assume they know what a person wants or expects from spiritual direction but should listen carefully to identify what people hope to accomplish through the spiritual direction conversation. Some individuals might not want spiritual direction at all but instead may want counseling, case management, or companionship. The best way to clarify expectations is to ask. A good opening question is, "How do you hope your relationship with God or others will be different as a result of spiritual direction?"

If the response to this question suggests that a person needs help identifying community resources, solving a behavioral problem, or grieving a death, the person may benefit more from another type of pastoral care. But if people ask for help learning to pray, clarifying God's role in their lives, or exploring the spiritual meaning of an event, dream, or relationship, spiritual direction may be the most appropriate form of care.

If the pastor determines a person is seeking spiritual direction rather than some other form of care, it can be helpful to categorize the concerns that led the person to seek direction. Typical concerns in spiritual direction include praying, finding forgiveness, growing closer to God, becoming more like Christ, and gaining a better understanding of particular spiritual experiences. Within these broad areas of concern, specific needs might include obtaining guidance in spiritual reading, detecting mediocrity or inner weakness, handling dry and difficult prayer, doing penance, discerning vocation, evaluating spiritual progress, and receiving support and accountability.[1] Brief and single-session spiritual direction is particularly suited to offering encouragement, challenging people, promoting healing and liberation, and suggesting new directions for spiritual life.[2]

FIGURE 1
The Stages of the First Session of Brief Spiritual Direction

Social (10 minutes)

Tasks
- Establish a relationship.
- Share personal information.
- Become comfortable talking with each other.

Transition (5 minutes)

Tasks
- Move from socializing to focusing on the directee's spiritual life.
- Begin with a prayer or silence, if the directee wishes.
- Introduce the storytelling stage.

Storytelling (20 minutes)

Tasks
- Allow the directee to tell what seems important about his or her spiritual life.
- Gather specific information about the directee's prayer life.
- Begin to identify the directee's primary ways of communicating with God.
- Begin to identify the hopes, dreams, and changes to be addressed.

Goal Setting (5 minutes)

Tasks
- Identify primary and secondary goals for the process of spiritual direction.
- Clarify the director's understanding of the directee's goals.

Reflection (15 minutes)

Tasks
- Highlight the strengths of the directee's spiritual life.
- Name the ways in which God is acting in the directee's life.
- Choose an appropriate response to God's presence and action.
- Identify resources for addressing the goals of spiritual direction.

Covenanting (5 minutes)

Tasks
- Review the work attended to in the first session.
- Decide whether future sessions are necessary.
- Make a covenant about future sessions.
- Clarify expectations for the direction relationship.
- Close the session with prayer.

Once it is clear that the person wants to engage in a spiritual direction conversation, the pastor begins to discern whether a long- or short-term approach is most appropriate. As discussed in chapter 3, the easiest way to determine whether spiritual direction should be brief is to ask directees how many times (or for how long a period) they expect to meet. A short-term approach is most appropriate with people who expect fewer than five spiritual direction sessions in a year.

Not everyone who seeks spiritual direction, of course, will be ready for this type of pastoral care. Brief spiritual direction, especially, is not for everyone; to be successful, it requires an active, committed stance from both the director and the directee. For this reason, several types of directees may not benefit from brief spiritual direction. They include people with little motivation to deepen their relationship with God and those who expect spiritual direction to "fix" their relationship with God. In addition, people who find it difficult in general to establish trusting relationships, and those with a history of failed spiritual direction relationships, are probably not good candidates for brief spiritual direction.

MEETING FOR THE FIRST TIME

The first session of brief spiritual direction lasts about an hour, although the participants may decide in advance to spend more time in the initial session, especially if it is to be the only meeting. Regardless of length, conversation during a first session tends to unfold in six overlapping stages: a social stage, a transition stage, a storytelling stage, a goal-setting stage, a reflection stage, and a housekeeping stage.

Two challenges mark the first session of brief spiritual direction. First is a tendency to oversimplify the directee's concerns. Second, directors may attempt to accomplish too much in too little time. Pastors would do well to remind themselves and their directees of these concerns at the beginning of a first session—during the social stage or by the end of the transition stage. Naming these challenges at the beginning of the process can help director and directee pay attention to these seductions and thus prevent or dissipate the sense of frustration they can introduce to a first session of brief spiritual direction.

The social stage of the first session establishes or confirms the connection between director and directee. These two people are either beginning to know each other or, if they are already acquainted, to "catch up" with each other's lives. The social stage is essential because a spiritual direction conversation focuses on an intimate facet of people's lives; to be as honest and vulnerable as the conversation requires, the director and directee must be comfortable with each other. Thus, the social stage is marked by an almost casual "getting to know you" dialogue typical in many North American relationships. The director and directee may disclose family and career information, geographical roots, educational background, faith commitments, and other personal facts. The director should also affirm the confidentiality of the information shared, specifically naming any limits to confidentiality (such as the requirement to report the abuse of children or the elderly).

It is important to note that the social stage is not a one-way exchange, with directees offering details about their lives to the director the way a patient describes symptoms to a physician. Spiritual directors also speak about themselves, including their interests, experiences, and faith commitments. This is one way to establish mutuality in the relationship. At this stage, the director may also inquire about the events of the directee's day; this allows people to identify recent experiences and emotions that could keep them from focusing wholly on the spiritual direction conversation.

As important as the social stage can be, however, the director should not allow it to dominate the session. Long-term spiritual direction can allow tremendous space for social exchange and deepening the relationship between director and directee; brief spiritual direction, on the other hand, requires the conversation to move as quickly as possible to the heart of the matter: the directee's relationship with God. For this reason, directors providing brief spiritual direction limit the social stage to less than ten minutes of the first session, using their pastoral authority to shift the conversation into the transition stage between socializing and storytelling.

Some directees make this shift naturally, but it is more likely that the director will need to make an intentional transition from routine conversation to dialogue focused on God's presence and action in the directee's life. Prayer is a natural way to make this shift, but not all directees will be comfortable praying with a director early in a first session. For that reason, I tend to enter the transitional stage by saying something like, "It's good to get to know you a little, and I do want to learn more about you. But we've gotten together this afternoon to focus on your spiritual life; for me, spiritual direction has to do with listening for God's presence and action in your everyday life and doing what we can to 'tend the holy' in your relationships and in your daily living. Would it be OK to move in that direction now?"

Next, I invite the directee to speak about her hopes for spiritual direction by saying something like, "Tell me what you hope spiritual direction will add to your life with God" or "What caused you to ask for spiritual direction at this point in your life?" The answers to questions like these allow the director to begin identifying the directee's goals for the spiritual direction conversation.

For example, when Deacon Juan Gonzalez asked Wendy these transitional questions, she said, "When you talked about praying with Scripture on Sunday, I connected immediately. I realized that I've always been better at using my imagination in prayer than in using words. So I hope you can help me figure out two experiences I've had in prayer this year. At first, I thought they were weird and too strange to share with anyone, but given what you said Sunday I think you'll understand." Her answer helped Juan understand that Wendy was trying to make sense of recent prayer experiences and perhaps to clarify what sort of prayer God was calling her to at this point in her life. This clarification allowed him to move into the storytelling stage of the first session with a better understanding of the conversation's purpose.

If directors sense a person is open to praying with them, the transition stage can be closed by asking, "Would it be good to begin with prayer or silence?" If the person wants to begin with prayer, the director can offer a short prayer giving thanks for the opportunity to pause and listen together for the voice of God, followed by a brief silence. If the person prefers to begin with silence rather than spoken prayer, the director can invite the person to close the time of silence by saying "Amen" when she is ready to speak. Asking the directee to close the time of silence ensures that she remains in control of the amount of time allotted to silence. (On occasion, a directee may choose to spend an entire session sitting in silence.) When the time of silence is complete, the director invites the person to move into storytelling.

TELLING STORIES AND IDENTIFYING GOALS

For much of the church's history, spiritual direction focused primarily on prayer. Directors attended carefully to the sorts of prayer their directees engaged in, their experiences during prayer, their sense of God's answers to their prayers, and their own emotional responses to their prayer life and to God's action in their lives. Today prayer remains important to spiritual direction, but pastoral caregivers also recognize the importance of attending to people's *stories* about their spiritual journeys and their relationships with God. Often, attending to the initial story can be more fruitful for the directee than focusing immediately on prayer, especially in brief spiritual direction.

Thus, in the first session of brief spiritual direction, the director listens to the directee's initial stories to establish a relationship with the person and to identify the unspoken hopes, dreams, and goals the person might have for the spiritual direction relationship. Hearing these initial stories is an important step toward clarifying the purpose of the brief spiritual direction relationship. Only by listening carefully to the person's stories can the director begin to sort through what events or experiences are important—and which are peripheral—to the process of spiritual guidance that will take place in just a few conversations.

Storytelling serves at least two purposes in brief spiritual direction. First, it allows directees to speak directly about what is foremost on their minds, telling at least part of the story of their relationship with God. Second, it provides directors with a glimpse of the changes directees are seeking in their relationships with God. These changes point toward the directee's goals for the spiritual direction process. By listening to the story, the director begins to learn details about the directee's spiritual life, including the specific hurts, hopes, and needs the person has brought to spiritual direction.

Two questions based on the work of William Barry and William Connolly can provide fruitful starting points for the storytelling stage.[3] (In fact, reflective and self-aware directees might find that these two questions provide good, brief spiritual direction in and of themselves.)

First, the director might ask, "Can you describe the ways in which you listen to God when you pray?" The directee's answer helps the director identify the types of prayer the person is practicing, and the question might also elicit a glimpse of the directee's primary attitudes toward God. For example, a person might say, "Oh, God always responds to prayer immediately; I feel it in my soul" or "I don't expect answers; I know God is too busy to answer our prayers." The first response suggests an immediate and affective awareness of God in the moment; the second, a distant and perhaps intellectualized relationship to God.

Many people stop short at this question about listening to God. *Listening* is not something they associate with prayer; their prayer life consists primarily of *telling* God about their hopes, fears, wants, and needs. When working with those who do not listen to God in prayer, the director can ask people to imagine what it might be like to listen to God. The directee's response provides a glimpse into the person's primary images of and attitudes toward God. Alternatively, the director can ask people who do not listen in prayer to identify and explore a time when God communicated with them. Listening to their response helps the director understand how people perceive God to act in their lives. The question also causes directees to identify a time when they *were* listening to God and to consider what difference their listening made in their relationship with God.

After exploring how the directee does (or doesn't) listen to God in prayer, the director's second question can be, "When you do listen to God, what do you typically share (or what do you imagine sharing) with God about what you've heard?" Attending to responses to this question can help the director both identify the level of intimacy between a directee and God and monitor the emotional tone of the directee's prayer life. When Deacon Juan asked Wendy this question, for example, she said, "Oh, I immediately give thanks to God for talking to me. Sometimes I cry a little—you know, tear up—but I keep my emotion to myself. God already knows what I'm feeling." Wendy's answer suggested to Juan that her relationship with God was not very intimate; while she tried to respond in ways that would please God, she didn't share the deepest parts of herself. (Of course, working from a not-knowing position, Juan would gently question Wendy about his observations to see if he was on target or had misinterpreted her description of her experience.)

Other helpful questions during the storytelling stage of brief spiritual direction include the following:

- In what ways have you noticed God at work in your life recently?
- What are your habits in prayer?
- What events in your life awakened your desires to become closer to God?
- What parts of the story of your journey of faith are the most important right now? Which ones do I need to know to understand how you've come to the place you're at now?

As the directee tells the story, the director listens intently and prayerfully—leaning forward, keeping his posture relaxed and open, making appropriate eye contact, and responding with verbal and nonverbal cues that indicate interest, understanding, and a desire to hear more. At the same time, the director is listening on an interior level to hear the presence, voice, and prompting of God within the conversation. Finely honed listening skills are among the best tools in spiritual direction; directors who feel deficient in this area may consult a number of introductory pastoral care, pastoral counseling, or spiritual direction texts to sharpen and expand their ability to listen.

While the preceding paragraphs might suggest that spiritual guides "direct" the storytelling stage, it is important to remember that directees need to be able to speak freely about whatever is in their hearts. Directors who speak more often than they listen during the storytelling stage may not be allowing appropriate space for directees to tell their stories. Together, the storytelling and goal-setting stages last about thirty minutes during a first, hour-long session of brief spiritual direction.

As the spiritual director listens to the story being told, she should note the yearnings and motivations—stated and unstated, conscious and unconscious—that are part of the narrative. These yearnings help the director and the directee identify the particular goals of a spiritual direction relationship—what the directee hopes will change as a result of spiritual direction. For some people, the goals of spiritual direction become clear when they state their reasons for seeing a director—to learn new ways of prayer, for example, or to understand a particular experience with God. For others, the goals of spiritual direction will be less evident immediately; the director will need to ferret them out through careful listening and thoughtful questions.

Wendy Grey, for example, said she was seeking spiritual direction "to talk about her prayer life." This is a vague goal, and it does not provide Deacon Juan with a helpful focus for listening to Wendy's story. As Wendy spoke, however, he discerned that her prayers did not include much intimacy with God. When he asked Wendy if this were an accurate understanding, she agreed. "So," Juan said, "would it be fair to say that becoming more intimate with God is one of the reasons you want to talk about your prayer life?"

"Yes, I think so," Wendy said. "But that's less important than figuring out what sorts of prayer work best for me—like praying with my imagination rather than with words."

Here, Wendy clearly told Juan that becoming more intimate with God was not her first priority in spiritual direction. Rather, she wanted first to discover what methods of prayer worked best for her. Juan did not assume he understood what this meant, however; instead, he asked, "Help me understand what's important about figuring out what sorts of prayer 'work' best for you."

"I think that's important so I can communicate more directly with God," Wendy said, "so I can feel more connected to Christ and know more clearly what his will is for my life, today and in the future."

Juan nodded. "So more intimacy would be OK," he said, "but first you want to feel more confident that you hear Christ's voice in your life and understand what he's calling you to in terms of daily living and long-term goals that are faithful to his vision for you?"

"Exactly," Wendy nodded. "Can you help me with that?"

Together, Wendy and Juan identified two primary goals for spiritual direction—finding an effective way for her to hear God's voice in her life and discerning whether she heard God's voice accurately. A secondary goal—increasing her level of intimacy with God—seems to be more important to Juan than to Wendy, although she has agreed it would be beneficial. While addressing the primary and secondary goals might happen simultaneously, Juan is clear that Wendy believes she needs to hear God more clearly before she can work at a more intimate relationship with God. Thus, he has clarified his immediate role and purpose in this particular conversation and spiritual direction relationship.

REFLECTING ON THE STORY

Once the initial story has been heard and goals have been established for the process of spiritual direction, the director's attention turns to reflection on the presence of God in the directee's life. Here the task is threefold: to highlight the perceived strengths of the directee's spirituality, to name the ways in which God seems to be acting in the directee's life, and to discern an appropriate response to God's presence and action. In general, at least fifteen minutes of an hour-long session are allocated for this process.

Reflection begins with the director highlighting some of the strengths of the directee's spiritual life. Complimenting aspects of people's life with God reminds them that no matter how difficult prayer might be or how distant God might feel, they still maintain some influence over their spiritual lives and that parts of their relationship with God are going well. Recognizing these facts can be helpful as the conversation turns to reflection on God's presence in the directee's life and in the spiritual direction session.

Compliments from the director have the most impact when they highlight aspects of the divine-human relationship over which the directee has some influence. For example, the director might compliment an ability to be intimate and vulnerable with God, a disciplined approach to prayer, a commitment to corporate worship, or a careful balance of contemplative prayer and social action. Deacon Juan might compliment Wendy Grey's awareness that she hears God most clearly through imaginative prayer rather than through discursive prayer. He might also compliment her commitment to discerning God's will for her life rather than assuming she knows what God wants for her.

Most of the time, offering compliments that highlight spiritual strengths is not difficult. But occasionally a director might fail to identify strengths in a person's life with God. While this situation might say more about a director's lack of imagination than about the quality of a directee's spiritual life, one particular strength can be highlighted for every directee: the decision to seek spiritual direction. Asking for guidance in one's spiritual life is an action that demonstrates a desire to grow closer to God and to be intentional about spiritual growth—both of which can be important strengths to highlight in the first session of short-term spiritual direction.

After briefly highlighting strengths, the director begins to name the ways God seems to be acting in the directee's life. This naming can occur in two steps. First, the director and directee might sit in silence for a few moments, after which the director can ask, "As you reflect on our conversation so far, where do you see God at work in your life right now?" A director may be anxious to offer personal reflections on the directee's story, but first attending to the directee's perceptions of God's action in her life allows the director to identify and focus on those manifestations of the Divine that the directee finds significant. Sometimes this is all that is required in order to name the ways in which God is acting in the directee's life.

At other times, especially if the directee's reflections are quite different from the director's observations, a second step is required. This consists of the director's offering—tentatively, from a posture of curiosity and not knowing—his or her own perceptions of God's action in the directee's life. Here, a director must reflect on and articulate his or her interior awareness of God's presence in the directee's life, which he or she noticed during the storytelling stage. These reflections are best offered as "wonderings," or things the director is curious about, rather than as things the director "knows." This way, the directee is free to accept or reject the director's observations.

For example, Deacon Juan might reflect on Wendy's life with God by saying, "I'm wondering if one place God is at work in your life is in your desire to clarify what sorts of prayer might be helpful to you. That very yearning might be God calling you to a renewed prayer life—like God stirring things up a little inside of you so your relationship together can reach new levels of intimacy." Once Wendy responds to this observation, Juan might say further, "I'm also curious if the fact that I lectured on prayer with Scripture last Sunday—and the fact that you were able to be there for the class—might suggest God is working in your life through your church community and through other people as much as in your private prayers."

Note that Juan keeps his comments focused on Wendy's goals for spiritual direction: hearing God's voice in her life, discerning the message, and increasing intimacy with God. Pastors and others providing spiritual direction assume God is working in people's lives to create a more abundant life; indeed, God often is already at work in ways that will help directees reach their goals for spiritual direction. By keeping reflections focused on the goals directees have named, directors help keep the spiritual direction relationship brief and focused on immediate concerns.

Of course, if a director discerns that God is at work in someone's life in ways that are opposed to the goals the directee has identified, this discrepancy must be noted and addressed. In such situations, a long-term approach to spiritual direction might be more suitable than a short-term approach. A long-term approach may also be indicated when an individual holds religious ideas or understandings that the spiritual director perceives as distorted or harmful. Brief spiritual direction may not be the best venue for the careful and honest conversation required to address these concerns in a responsible way. Certainly, directors who sense a significant conflict between their own theologies and those of the person seeking spiritual guidance may choose to refer the person to another director for care.

The task of spiritual direction, however, does not rest solely in identifying God's presence in a person's life. Action from the directee must follow; the director's assumption that God is at work to make each person's life more abundant is paired with an assumption that spiritual direction should help people collaborate with God's life-giving actions. Thus, the reflection stage of a spiritual direction session—whether the meeting is the first or fortieth—is not complete until the director and directee have discerned an appropriate and intentional response to God's presence and action in the directee's life.

A simple way to do this is to ask directees how they would like to respond to God. Typically, people can imagine several appropriate responses in keeping with their own spirituality, religious tradition, and level of intimacy with God. The director should encourage such personal responses while taking care to ensure they are *specific, small, simple,* and *behavioral.* For example, a directee who says, "I'll give thanks to God" has named a general rather than a specific response; it would be better to say, "I will offer a prayer of thanksgiving tonight before I go to bed." A directee who says, "I will undertake a ten-day silent retreat in Australia to listen for God's will for my life," has not named a simple or small response to God's presence and action; a smaller, simpler response would be a one-day retreat at home to discern if a ten-day retreat would be helpful. A directee who says, "In response to God, I will feel happier at work," has named not a behavior but a feeling over which he has no control; a more appropriate response in keeping with the affective desire would be to smile at her coworkers and say an interior prayer for their happiness as they arrive at the office.

In general, a response to God's presence and action should be stated as the presence of some behavior rather than the absence of some behavior. For example, a directee might resolve to "tell the truth to my brother" rather than to "stop lying to relatives." The best responses require the directee to *do* something rather than to feel or think something; they also build on something the directee is already doing rather than requiring an entirely new behavior.

Often, the director's primary role at this point will be to help directees simplify and focus their responses to God. For example, a directee might say, "Seeing how God has protected me makes me want to dedicate my life totally to serving Christ." This response is behavioral, but it is not small, simple, or specific. To sharpen this response, a director might ask, "What's one small way you could dedicate your life to serving Christ during the next day or two?" By focusing on a more specific way of dedicating her life to Christ's service, the directee might decide to practice a daily act of compassion toward a coworker or to offer a prayer of dedication during her usual morning devotions.

MAKING A COVENANT FOR CARE

Once directees have identified an appropriate response to God's work in their lives, the first session of brief spiritual direction ends. The director might briefly review the work that has been attended to during the session: establishing a relationship between director and directee, hearing the directee's story, choosing a goal for spiritual direction, identifying God's presence in the directee's life, and discerning an appropriate response to the unique way God has been at work in the life of the directee. This is also a good time to reaffirm the confidentiality of the information shared during the session. Once these activities are complete, it is time to decide if there will be a second session.

In general, this decision belongs to the directee. If the person does not want a second session, the director should clarify whether the directee is welcome to make another appointment sometime in the future. If the person desires an ongoing relationship, the director and directee may covenant to meet three to five more times, reviewing their progress during the final session and making a deliberate decision about whether to continue. At the time a covenant is made, directors should clarify their expectations for the relationship—whether they expect the person to participate in daily prayer, for example, or weekly communion; how much time will elapse between meetings; the director's availability between sessions; and any commitments to hold each other in mutual prayer.

No matter how many times a pastor and directee meet, it is important at the conclusion of the spiritual direction process to review the growth that occurred for the directee, to name the spiritual themes or metaphors that dominated the process, to allow time for both director and directee to speak from the heart about what the relationship has meant to them, and to give thanks together in prayer for the relationship and God's presence in it. Each session should be closed with prayer— either a time of silence ended with a simple "Amen" or a spoken prayer. I like to invite directees to end each session with prayer unless they prefer that I pray.

CONCLUSION: LOOKING BEYOND THE FIRST SESSION

The first session of brief spiritual direction focuses on directees' thoughts, emotions, and behaviors presented in the form of a story. Once the story (or at least one version of it) has been told, the director helps directees relate the thoughts, emotions, and behaviors present in the story to their awareness of and responses to the ways in which the Holy One has entered their lives. During the first session, the director seeks to attend to how God is already at work in people's lives and how they can cooperate with the changes God is working. Brief pastoral counseling recognizes there are always exceptions to a problem; likewise, brief spiritual direction recognizes God is always present in each person's life. The issue is for the director and directee not to resolve a spiritual difficulty but to identify God's work already taking place and find ways to collaborate with it.

This practice of clarifying directees' needs and discerning God's presence is the primary task of brief spiritual direction. In fact, helping directees notice that God is present and at work in their lives can sometimes be enough to relieve the anxiety that brought them to spiritual direction in the first place. Some of the time, however, more action is required. In these cases, both the long tradition of spiritual direction and the theory of brief pastoral counseling can provide the director with guidance for proceeding. The next two chapters explore interventions from Christian spiritual traditions and from the practice of brief pastoral counseling that can be adapted for use in brief spiritual direction.

5

TAKING ACTION:
TECHNIQUES FROM
BRIEF PASTORAL COUNSELING

A major premise of this book is that the assumptions and ideas behind brief pastoral counseling can help the pastor take action in brief spiritual direction. As discussed in chapter 3, many concepts from the theory of short-term pastoral counseling are not unique—and certainly are not new approaches to spiritual direction—but highlight important aspects of brief care in any situation. If spiritual direction is viewed as a specific type of conversation, the techniques discussed in this chapter give shape to that conversation, especially when it occurs during just a few meetings between a pastor and a person seeking spiritual guidance.

Four broad concepts inform the practice of brief spiritual direction: attending to the facts of everyday life, focusing on possibilities in the present and future, tailoring care to the individual, and persevering in the face of boredom or frustration. In addition to discussing these concepts, this chapter suggests specific interventions from the practice of brief pastoral counseling that a pastor may adapt for use with people seeking spiritual direction. These interventions include identifying and building on exceptions, deconstructing directees' ideas, identifying competencies and resources, mapping the influence of particular experiences, and using the "Miracle Question" to set goals.

Before proceeding, however, I must confess some inner resistance to the idea of talking about "techniques" and "interventions" for the practice of spiritual direction. Using these terms seems to reflect a mechanistic, problem-solving approach to spiritual growth, and I do not think successful spiritual direction is about technique or interventions. Spiritual direction is an art, not a technology, and spiritual growth occurs on God's schedule through the actions of the Holy Spirit, not through the application of human wisdom or therapeutic techniques. Some "tools" from brief therapy lend themselves to the practice of brief spiritual direction, but the most important tool for spiritual direction of any type is careful and active listening from a not-knowing position. Without well-developed listening skills and an ability to draw people deeper into their stories, the pastor or spiritual director will find it difficult to provide effective spiritual care.

Nonetheless, pastors and others with a gift for spiritual direction can make the most of brief encounters by intentionally incorporating concepts and techniques from brief therapy into their spiritual direction conversations. Those concepts and techniques are discussed below, beginning with a focus on everyday life.

WORKING WITH EVERYDAY LIFE

"Mountaintop" experiences of God and romantic ideas about what it means to be spiritual sometimes motivate people to seek spiritual direction. Often such people want to talk only about sublime experiences from the past; sometimes they limit conversation to generic, idealized descriptions of life with God. Neither approach is likely to put enough on the plate to satisfy a spirit hungry for a taste of God; attempting to satisfy spiritual hunger by focusing on broad generalities or past epiphanies can be as frustrating as a hungry teenager trying to satisfy her appetite with water and dried beans.

The practitioner of brief spiritual direction recognizes that spiritual growth comes about by focusing on everyday thoughts and mundane behaviors. Spiritual progress is best measured by changes in daily experience, not by isolated mystical or emotional experiences. Sometimes, in fact, the people whose spirits are the most mature appear most ordinary to those around them.

When a director or directee fails to recognize that spiritual maturity is best discerned by attending to a person's behaviors in daily life, spiritual direction conversations can become otherworldly—so focused on heaven, as the old saying goes, that they're no earthly good. Such conversations allow directees to detach their faith from the realities of their lives. It is these sorts of conversations that have led Episcopal priest Alan Jones to advocate for "non-spiritual, non-direction." True spiritual direction, he writes, "lies in our uncovering the obvious in our lives and in realizing that everyday events are the means by which God tries to reach us."[1]

The path to spiritual understanding and growth, then, is found in the dirty diapers and exhaust fumes and complicated relationships and cold, sandy swimsuits of our lives. Everything we encounter, everything around us—our families, our habits, our smallest choices, the cultures and economic conditions that shape us, the friends who surround us, the books we read, the media that form our attitudes—everything has the capacity to serve as a pager or instant text message through which God calls us to become something more. Sometimes life can feel like scrolling through endless pages on the World Wide Web—when suddenly a new window pops up, providing a link to a holy (and wholly) new possibility or reality that has been there all along but that we did not know how to access.

This interpenetration of the sacred and the mundane is one reason it is essential in brief spiritual direction to return again and again to directees' experiences of daily life—especially their experiences of relationship with others. The quality of people's relationships can be a good measure of their spiritual life; as Jones has written, "Our relationship with God is bound up with our relationship with one another and with the whole created order."[2] In the Orthodox tradition of spiritual direction, spiritual guides take a dual focus: attending to both what is happening within a person's heart and mind and what is happening behaviorally between people and those who share their daily lives.[3] Both the inner and the outer experiences of everyday life have spiritual dimensions.

Attending to everyday experience in brief spiritual direction is not difficult. The key is asking directees to reflect contemplatively on their daily lives, looking and listening for indications of God's presence and direction amid shopping for groceries, managing employees, cooking dinner, and walking the dog. This sort of reflection—done prayerfully and with an intention to be open to the changes God is bringing—is a requirement of successful spiritual direction, short- or long-term.

One method of guiding contemplative reflection consists of focusing, as Robert Morneau suggests, on three phenomena: the disposition of directees (what they expect of life, how they approach the "givens" or finitude of their situations, the moods or emotions coloring their perceptions), the experiences of directees (what happens to, with, and through them in daily life), and the process by which directees reflect on experience (including the interplay of a person's disposition and the content of his or her reflection).[4] The complex patterns created by these three elements can provide rich fodder for spiritual growth, and the quickest way to get them dancing together is to ask genuinely curious questions about a directee's worldview and experiences, and the meanings he or she perceives in those experiences.

For example, one Sunday evening I took communion to a parishioner in the hospital. As I waited for the elevator, a woman pointed to the communion set and asked, "Bringing the Eucharist to someone?" I nodded. "That's good," she said as we got on the elevator. "Communion is important. I always ask for communion when I'm sick. I don't take it otherwise."

"Why is that?" I asked.

"I don't know," she said, punching the button for her floor. "There's just something healing about it. I think that's what the Eucharist is for, really: healing the body and the soul."

"But you only take it when you're sick?" I asked. She nodded.

As we rode in silence, a question formed in my head. "May I ask you a personal question?" I said. She agreed, and we looked into each other's eyes for a few seconds. "I wonder," I said finally, "if you'd heal in other ways if you took communion even when your body is fine?"

The elevator opened at her floor. She stepped out but used her hand to stop the door from closing. "Why did you ask that?" she said with a note of curiosity in her voice.

"I don't know," I said. "I just wonder what sort of relationship God wants with you if you always experience communion as healing? I wonder what might happen if you came home for supper a little more often."

Tears came to her eyes. "I think I just got a hand-delivered invitation," she said. "Supper with my Savior any day I care to stop by." Then she let the elevator doors close.

In general, I don't recommend (or often practice!) this sort of "hit-and-run" spiritual guidance, but I think my questions served to clarify the woman's disposition toward communion, draw her attention to her experience in the moment, and stimulate reflection on the meaning of her elevator ride with a nosy stranger. With her closing comment, she clearly suggested that she felt God's presence in our conversation. If I were in a spiritual direction relationship with her, I might follow up with more questions about times that she has experienced God's presence in daily life, whether those experiences might be "healing moments" even though the sacrament was not present, and what it might mean for her relationship with God that she has limited Christ's healing presence to times when she is physically ill.

Questions like these, though simple, can be the most effective interventions in spiritual direction, especially when they spark reflection on the experiences of daily life. Some questions a director might consider asking include the following:

- What is God's call in this situation?
- What challenges and opportunities are offered?
- What healing or growth might God be inviting?

- What difference will a particular decision make in day-to-day life, in the ways a person knows God, or in the ways a person prays?
- How might reflection on a particular experience change a person in the future?[5]

FOCUSING ON POSSIBILITIES

Short-term pastoral counseling not only makes the ordinary times in people's lives the "stuff" of therapeutic reflection but also tends to focus on what is possible in the present and the future rather than spending energy on what has happened in the past. Brief counseling emphasizes the first, small steps to a transformed life here and now. Likewise, brief spiritual direction focuses on the present and the future, looking for ways that God is creating possibilities in a person's life at this moment.

For this reason, brief spiritual directors must affirm but also set aside a directee's previous experiences of and assumptions about God. Focusing on the past—both past experiences and past understandings of God—can limit the spiritual direction conversation to familiar territory rather than allowing it to follow new paths toward different and perhaps unimagined possibilities. Pastors providing brief spiritual direction will find that people's attention must be turned continually away from a focus on problems and the past to focus instead on what is possible with God.

This is not just "positive thinking" dressed up in religious language, nor is it simply a change in attitude. The focus on possibilities in brief spiritual direction reflects—and can create and promote—the belief that God can and does change a person's entire being. To be successful in brief spiritual direction, the director must communicate both trust in God's presence and a belief that the directee can grow closer to God. Above all, the director must believe that directees have the resources and capacities to address the concerns that brought them to spiritual direction in the first place. Those concerns are best addressed by acting in the present and future rather than stewing about the past.

Emily, for example, sought spiritual direction after a car accident left her permanently disabled. She was no longer able to ride horses, jog in the park near her house, or roughhouse with her children—the primary activities through which she had experienced God's presence and care in the past. Quiet and stillness had never been conduits of spiritual insight for Emily; God spoke to her most clearly when she was most active, and due to her new physical limitations she despaired of ever experiencing God's presence again.

Emily asked me for help identifying God's presence in her new life, not for help grieving her losses or adjusting to her injury. Because of this, each time she reflected on past experiences of God, I gently returned her to the present by saying something like, "I know you miss the feeling of God being close to you as you ran through the park, but running isn't an option anymore. What can you do now that is most like running?"

By repeatedly focusing on possibilities in the present and future, Emily was able to experience God's presence in slow walks with her children and by contemplatively "entering into" the experience of horseback riding as she watched her husband train his mare. Gradually, she began to notice the continual activity of creation even at those times most people considered the world still or quiet. By "praying with" the wind in the trees, the whir of cicadas, and the rumbling of thunder, Emily felt God's active presence in places she had never perceived it before. As our spiritual direction relationship progressed, Emily spoke less of the past and more of the present and future; this allowed me to use the identification of exceptions (see below), rather than a focus on possibilities, as my primary intervention in spiritual direction.

TAILORING CARE TO THE INDIVIDUAL

In brief pastoral counseling, the goals and content of therapy are determined by the counselee. People are allowed to be the experts on their own lives rather than relying on the therapist to render an expert judgment or diagnosis and then develop a treatment plan. In brief spiritual direction, too, the directee is the expert; the work focuses on the directee's agenda, not the agenda of the director, no matter how much "expertise" the director brings to the table. This idea is related to the not-knowing attitude discussed in chapter 2.

Tailoring care in this way is accomplished by thoroughly attending first to the individual's experiences, language for God, and unique ways of relating to the holy. Only after exploring these personal characteristics does the brief spiritual director turn attention to Scripture, tradition, or the director's knowledge of the spiritual life and his experience with other directees. As British spiritual director Gordon Jeff writes: "Try to respond to the person concerned as a person. Don't think out how you are going to 'answer' their question; simply talking it through may enable them to find their own answer. Stay with their experiences and feelings, rather than quoting Bible texts at them or using theological language, which may mean something to you (does it?!) but will probably mean nothing to them."[6]

In my work with Emily, it would have been easy to recommend that she begin practicing contemplative methods for experiencing God, such as centering prayer or noticing the presence of God. After all, these are the methods that work best for me; in practical terms, her limited mobility suggested spiritual practices focused on "being still"; and most classic texts on spirituality point toward contemplative awareness during times of quiet as a foundation of the spiritual life. But by attending to Emily's individual experience, I kept myself focused on helping her notice God's presence in her most active moments; this in turn helped me avoid prescribing spiritual practices for which she was perhaps poorly suited. In addition, noticing that Emily, despite her education and long association with the church, never used "church words" or academic theological language to describe her experiences of God helped me keep my own language about spiritual experience concrete and personal rather than abstract, intellectual, and impersonal.

PERSEVERANCE

Another reason that brief pastoral counselors tailor care to the individual lies in two assumptions: change is always happening in people's lives, and dramatic change can happen quickly. In a similar way, practitioners of brief spiritual direction assume spiritual changes are always in process and can happen quickly. Nonetheless, God does not always act with speed, and often a significant amount of time is necessary to discern accurately God's action in an individual's life. For that reason (as ironic as it might sound), brief spiritual direction requires patience and perseverance. Some directees will feel bored and frustrated when God seems to be moving slowly; such times may lead others to begin doubting God's presence and action.

In these situations, spiritual directors do two things: they model constancy, and—focusing on the stuff of everyday life—they emphasize the possibilities inherent in the present and future. Citing scriptural examples of God's slow and patient way of taking action—including the Exodus narratives, the literature of the Babylonian captivity, and the apostle Paul's observation that the entire cosmos is straining and groaning to give birth to a new reality—can help put God's seeming inaction into perspective.

Overall, however, perseverance in brief spiritual direction means attending to the meaning and significance the directee places on God's seeming inactivity. Perseverance also means helping the directee devise an honest, faithful response to the situation. If the person is bored or frustrated, use the boredom and frustration as the focus of spiritual direction. How does the boredom and frustration affect the way the directee perceives God? Has the directee shared his boredom and frustration with God? In what way is God calling him to wholeness through the experience of boredom and frustration? Again, the director should persevere in attending to the directee's experience and what it means in the person's life and relationship with God, both at the moment and in the future.

Frustration about God's lack of response to prayer led a directee named Shawn, for example, to seek guidance from Pastor Steve. After listening to the story of dry and fruitless prayer, Steve affirmed Shawn's frustration. Then he asked, "How have you expressed that frustration to God?"

Shawn was momentarily perplexed; sharing the frustration of unanswered prayer with God had never seemed like an option. "I guess I've been giving God the silent treatment," Shawn said. "I'm so pissed off that my life hasn't gotten better that I stopped talking to the person who's responsible for it."

Steve suggested that instead of remaining silent, Shawn might try praying about the frustration—not asking that it be removed, but expressing to God all of the attendant emotions: anger, fear of being abandoned by God, pain about the "stuckness" of life, and even the awkward feeling raised by saying those things to God. Steve also suggested that Shawn spend a week praying with Psalm 42, especially verses 2 and 9: "My soul thirsts for God, for the living God. When shall I come and behold the face of God? ... I say to God, my rock, 'Why have you forgotten me? Why must I walk about mournfully because the enemy oppresses me?'"

One week later, over lunch at a favorite Mexican restaurant, Steve asked Shawn how the frustration was going. "God still hasn't answered the prayer about changing my life," Shawn said. "But I'm a lot less frustrated by it—partly because God has responded to my prayers about being angry, sad, and afraid. In fact, I feel closer to God than I have in a long time—in Sunday worship and day by day. There's some comfort there that I hadn't noticed before; maybe it's the Holy Spirit bringing comfort. I guess 'talking it through' with God is as important as 'talking it through' with a boyfriend when there's a problem in our relationship."

The shift in Shawn's awareness of God's presence and response to prayer allowed Steve to identify and highlight an *exception* to Shawn's perception that God was not responding to prayer at all. Identifying and building on exceptions is the focus of the following section.

THERE'S ALWAYS AN EXCEPTION

At times, some directees will claim, like Shawn, that something *never* happens in their spiritual lives; they says things like, "God never responds to my prayers" or "I never experience grace when I need it." At other times, some directees will claim that a particular (bad) thing *always* happens in their spiritual lives: "Every time I share my true feelings with God, I get punished" or "I always fall asleep in the middle of praying."

When working with people for whom "always" and "never" are frequent refrains, spiritual directors can draw on the brief therapy practice of identifying exceptions to find times when the person's life is free of the difficulty that seems all pervading. For example, I had the following exchange with a man who claimed God was never active in his life:

> Director: God is never active in your life, huh? How would you know God was being active if it started to happen all of a sudden?
>
> Rob: I would just have a sense of being protected. I would see good things happening to me—I would feel hope.
>
> Director: When was the last time you felt protected or hopeful? What was the last good thing that happened to you?
>
> Rob: Well, I had a job interview. And the poem I'm working on is going really well. I don't worry so much about my bills right now.
>
> Director: So good things have happened, but God hasn't been active in your life?
>
> Rob: Well, I guess God has been present in my life. I just hadn't thought of those things being a part of God acting in my life.
>
> Director: I wonder if it would be helpful to spend some time reflecting on what kept you from noticing those things as a part of God's presence?

The focus of this spiritual direction conversation then moved from an unsolvable difficulty—God's inactivity, over which the directee had no control—to something the directee could influence—learning new ways to listen for the presence of God.

A director can build on exceptions by asking directees to reflect on what they did differently at the time of the exception—for example, did they pray at a different time than usual? Listen to God in a different way?

"Let go" of a desire to hear God's response? Sing the Lord's Prayer instead of saying it? Notice God's presence in nature instead of in church?

When an exception occurs, identifying what has been different than usual about a directee's thoughts, beliefs, and behaviors can help identify a way that God is acting in the person's life—calling the person to pray differently, for example, or to attend to experience differently. By noticing a change in his level of intimacy with God during communion, for example, one directee discerned that God was calling him toward a more contemplative and sacramental type of worship than he had practiced in the past. Brief spiritual directors encourage directees to be intentional about "doing something different"—repeating a behavior or way of thinking that somehow led to an exception in the person's experience of God.

TAKING BELIEFS APART AND BUILDING THEM UP AGAIN

The brief therapy practice of deconstruction—looking at the assumptions behind a person's thoughts and behaviors in order to see where they came from and how they are shaping experience—can also help in brief spiritual direction. But deconstruction alone is not sufficient. It must be followed by a reconstruction of belief by exploring how different assumptions about God, faith, and prayer might lead to different spiritual experiences. The back-and-forth, give-and-take process of deconstruction and reconstruction carries two potential benefits for directees. First, it can allow them to understand better where their beliefs came from and how those beliefs shape their relationship with God. Second, it can allow directees to consciously choose the beliefs that will shape their relationships with God and other people.

Deconstruction begins when spiritual directors glimpse (or have a hunch about) a belief or assumption that is shaping a directee's life with God. From a stance of not knowing, the director can gently point out the assumption and ask where it came from. The purpose of deconstruction is to help directees reflect on the experiences, people, texts, and other influences that helped establish the assumption being questioned. Deconstruction also seeks to identify concrete ways in which that assumption has influenced the person's spiritual life. For example, someone who assumes God will not approve of his sexual fantasies about his wife might identify two sources of this belief: a pastor who told him sex is only for the purpose of procreation, and New Testament letters that speak about fornication. As he reflects on the influence of his belief, he might realize that fear of God's disapproval keeps him from sharing his whole self in prayer—specifically, it keeps him from praying about his relationship with his wife and desire for greater intimacy with her.

Once the director and directee have deconstructed a particular belief or assumption, the process of reconstruction can begin. To initiate this process, the director can gently introduce an alternative belief and ask the directee to imagine how life with God would be different if the new belief had more influence in his life. For instance, the man who fears God's judgment about sexual fantasies might be asked to imagine that God created him with the capacity to fantasize about sex. Sometimes it is helpful to suggest an alternative belief that is radically different from—maybe even entirely opposed to—the assumption that was deconstructed. More often, it helps to introduce a belief that is just a little bit different from the assumption that has been influencing the directee.

Deconstruction and reconstruction are not necessarily long and involved processes; they can happen quite naturally in the course of a short conversation. For example, one woman talked at length in spiritual direction about what she wished for her relationships with her family. Her description was rich and detailed. But she finished by saying she didn't know how to ask God to help bring those changes about. As the director listened, she noted that the woman did not understand her yearning for change—and her verbal articulation of that yearning—as prayer. Here is how the conversation unfolded:

Mary: That's what I hope for every day. But I don't know how to ask God to help make those things happen.

Director: One way is to ask in prayer. And what you just described about the changes you hope for was a beautiful prayer about the things you want for your family.

Mary: Really? (*She begins to cry.*)

Director: Mary, I'm curious about your tears. What are they about?

Mary: I was always taught that you should only pray for other people. I guess I always thought it was wrong to pray for yourself. (*With this statement, Mary discloses an assumption that has shaped her relationship with God.*)

Director: I wonder where that idea came from? (*Here, the director begins the process of deconstruction by looking at the assumption—perhaps subconscious—that has shaped Mary's prayer life.*)

Mary: I don't know if anyone ever told me that; I just never heard my mother or my grandmother pray for themselves.

Director: So that idea's been around for a long time. How does it feel to think you just prayed for yourself? (*She nods, smiling.*) What would your life have been like if you had known as a child you could pray for yourself? (*This question initiates the process of reconstruction by asking Mary to imagine what her experience would be like if a different assumption influenced her prayer life.*)

Mary: (*Silence.*) I guess it would have felt a lot less alone. I would have known there was someone other than my family that I could rely on.

Director: Now that you know you're not alone, that there's someone else you can rely on to help you, how do you imagine your relationship to God changing? Or do you even want to start relating to God as if it's OK to pray for yourself? (*This question continues the reconstruction process, both by asking Mary to imagine how a different assumption might influence her experiences and by "checking out" whether this assumption is one she wants to choose to incorporate into her understanding of prayer and life with God.*)

Mary: I would have prayed a lot more!

The process of deconstruction and reconstruction ends with directees making a conscious decision to incorporate the new belief or assumption into their prayer lives and their spiritual activities. It is important that the director return to the subject in future sessions, both to see how a directee's relationship with God is changing as a result of the new belief and to hold the person accountable for the decision made during the process of reconstruction.

MAPPING MEANINGS AND ACTIONS

Sometimes it is not specific beliefs or assumptions that are influencing a person's spiritual life, but a particular experience or event. Frequently directors practicing brief spiritual direction are faced with a directee who has become fixated on an experience that seems to sum up his rela-

tionship with God or that motivates her desire to be in spiritual direction. At these times, directors might find it helpful to "map" the directee's
interpretation of the experience. Mapping occurs on two planes—the
meaning axis, which identifies the meanings a directee attributes to a
particular event, and the action axis, which identifies the impact of the
event on the directee's behaviors. In general, I encourage directors to
map the meaning of an experience before attempting to map the actions
that have resulted.

Mapping is accomplished through curiosity-driven questions directed
first toward one axis and then to the other. Questions along the meaning
axis seek to uncover the person's interior understandings of the special
event. For example, what does it mean that the event happened to this
person and not someone else? Why would God choose him for this particular experience? What responsibilities does the event place on the person? How has the experience changed the person's understandings of
God? Of self? Of prayer? Of worship? What does it say about the person
that she was open to the experience? What was God calling him to
through this experience? What prepared the person for this particular
event? What biblical character's experience was closest to this directee's
experience? How would the directee's spouse, parents, siblings, or
coworkers feel about the experience? How would they look at the
directee differently as a result of it? How might the person's desire to be
"special" in the eyes of God or friends distort her interpretation of the
event? In what ways might the directee's sinfulness prevent an accurate
understanding of God's presence and purpose in the experience?

Questions along the action axis seek to identify how the experience
has affected the directee's behaviors. How has her prayer life changed, for
example? Whom has he told about the experience? How does the person
relate differently to God and to other people as a result of the event?
What religious or spiritual activities have resulted from the experience?
What changes has the directee noticed in her thoughts, feelings, and
actions? How did he respond to the experience in prayer or ritual? How
does the directee hope to be different at work or church, in the choir or
at baseball practice, as a result of this experience? How does she imagine
other people have responded to similar experiences?

Every intervention in brief spiritual direction seeks to help people
identify God's presence and action in their lives and then to discern
appropriate responses to that presence or action. Mapping the meaning
of an experience can broaden and deepen a directee's understanding of a
particular experience of God's presence and action—including the
understanding of the ways in which God was present, the messages that
God intended to communicate, and how the directee's own hopes,

desires, and interpretations might be getting in the way of understanding God's intention for the experience. Mapping the action that has resulted from an experience of God helps the directee identify ways in which the experience has—consciously or subconsciously—initiated changes in behavior, thought, and relationships. Clarifying how actions already occurring are rooted in a particular experience of God may help a person discern an appropriate, intentional response to that experience. Any response should seek to keep directees in dialogue with God rather than assuming that a special experience is God's final word to them.

IDENTIFYING WHAT PEOPLE DO WELL AND WHO (OR WHAT) ELSE CAN HELP

In chapter 4, I encouraged directors to compliment directees for what they do to make a positive contribution to their spiritual lives, such as being involved in a congregation or setting time aside for prayer each day. Encouragement is a primary purpose of brief spiritual direction; people often ask to meet with a director simply to make sure they are "on track" in their relationship with God. Therefore, each session of brief spiritual direction should help directees better understand the unique strengths and resources that influence their spiritual lives. Ideally, compliments highlight behaviors that directees have some control over, such as the amount of time spent in devotional reading, bringing a contemplative awareness to their work in a soup kitchen, or learning a new type of prayer.

It's easy to identify strengths to compliment; the director simply notes actions that directees take to strengthen their relationship with God, paying special attention to those that directees deem important. Complimenting activities that directees consider insignificant usually has little impact; a person won't pay much attention to a compliment about his eyes if he thinks the size of his belly is the only thing others notice about him! Jane, for example, devotes at least an hour each day to individual Bible study and prayer; she considers this time essential to her relationship with God. She also spends three hours each week preparing to teach the single adults class at her church—but she considers this a duty of her role as elder rather than an act of worship. Complimenting her devotional time and encouraging her to broaden it by reading some systematic theology each day may carry more weight with Jane than praising her careful preparation for Sunday school. She doesn't think her teaching is important to her relationship with God, but she believes her prayer and reading affect it directly.

Compliments on a directee's behaviors are not sufficient, however. Spiritual growth doesn't happen in a vacuum, and it isn't an individual endeavor; it is shaped by the people and communities that surround a person. For this reason, it is important in brief spiritual direction to identify and tap into these outside resources; they have the potential to influence a directee's spiritual growth to a far greater extent than individual meetings with a spiritual director do. For this reason, the director should inquire about the people, communities, and institutions that a person thinks make a special, positive contribution to his or her spiritual life.

People often identify parents, grandparents, friends at church, or particular authors who influence their spirituality. Schoolmates, groups of friends, congregations, museums, libraries, artistic activities, or particular landscapes might also be resources for a person's spiritual growth or touchstones for their spiritual identities. Directors should inquire about people with whom directees feel a special spiritual connection; they should also ask about places or activities that nourish their directees' souls in ways they especially appreciate. For instance, a nurse I know consistently feels God's presence in the neonatal intensive care unit at his hospital; a businesswoman feels connected to God while bathing her two-year-old son; a musician feels nurtured and cared for during long walks by a river not far from his house; and a gay man highly values the communion table at his Baptist church, which welcomes him even when the Formica table in his parents' kitchen is off-limits because of his sexuality.

Once such outside influences and resources for spiritual growth and identity have been named, directors can ask directees what they will do to ensure that they have consistent interaction with these people, places, and institutions. Remaining in touch with these sources of spiritual nourishment can itself be a form of spiritual practice. One thing the practitioner of brief spiritual direction can do is hold people accountable for their relationships to the people and places that contribute to their spirituality in positive ways. The director might ask directees to make a monthly appointment with a museum, for example, or to commit to receiving communion weekly or to having coffee with their best friend twice a month.

When identifying other resources for spiritual growth, it is important to ask directees what people in their pasts have been influential. Even if the influential person—a grandfather, for example, or a former pastor—is deceased, he or she continues to be an influence that can be tapped for spiritual direction. This is because directees carry within themselves the wisdom of those who have been important spiritual influences; thoughtful directors can ask directees to reflect on the spiritual insights, gifts, or advice they received from these "ancestors in the faith," what spiritual wisdom these people knew about or saw in the directee that other people missed. Remembering these people on a regular basis and reflecting on the wisdom they have brought to the directee can also be a spiritual discipline. I have one directee, for example, who keeps snapshots of her "spiritual ancestors" on the homemade altar where she centers herself in prayer each morning and evening. "Seeing their faces each day reminds me who I am, where I come from, and how much God has gifted me," she says.

SOMETIMES IT TAKES A MIRACLE

Sometimes people seek spiritual direction because they feel spiritually off balance; something isn't right in their lives, although they might have trouble naming the source of their discomfort. Often this reflects an experience of spiritual desolation (see chapter 7). Such directees typically begin the first session by saying something like, "I don't really know why I'm here" or "For some reason, I just felt drawn to talking to you." By allowing them to tell their story, the director might be able to clarify the reasons they have asked for guidance. But sometimes identifying a goal for spiritual direction can be elusive, even after a long period of listening, prayer, and discernment.

To clarify the goal of a spiritual direction conversation, directors can borrow and adapt the "Miracle Question" used in brief psychotherapy. The Miracle Question is a way of helping directees imagine what sort of spiritual changes will make a difference to them at a particular time in their lives. Before asking the question, the director should encourage directees to close their eyes and relax, breathing deeply and clearing their minds. Then the director says:

> Imagine that you go to bed tonight feeling the full weight of what you are struggling with. You are confused (or empty or struggling). But during the night, while you are asleep, Jesus comes to your side and performs a miracle. Your struggle is over; the discomfort is resolved; it has melted away. When you wake up in the morning, what would be different? What would be the first sign that a miracle had happened? What would you do differently? What would you feel differently? Who else would notice? How would they know?

For example, Harry was an aging widower who felt restless and dissatisfied but did not see a link between these feelings and his devotional life. He responded to the Miracle Question by sitting in silence and then saying, "When I opened my eyes, I would feel a moment of thankfulness.

I would know God was blessing me in that very moment, and I would respond by saying, 'Thank you!' in my heart. I wouldn't turn on the radio or television; instead, I would let the silence of the house and the sounds of the birds speak to me while I washed my face and ate breakfast. I would do some yoga stretches as a way of honoring my body. And all through the day, I would whisper that prayer: 'Thank you!'"

Harry's spiritual director used the content of his miracle to encourage a sort of spiritual practice different from his usual weekly worship and occasional reading of Scripture. "As I listened to your miracle," she said, "it sounded like you're being called to the prayer of thanksgiving. And silence seems to be a part of that for you—savoring the day as it unfolds, noticing what you have to be thankful for, not distracting yourself with noise or worries. What do you think about trying to do some of that even though the miracle hasn't happened yet?"

Harry decided he would begin each day with silence, alternating day by day between yoga in the backyard and a walk around the block. While he exercised, he would notice things for which he was grateful. He would not read or listen to the television or radio, and after washing up, he would offer a morning prayer of thanksgiving and praise. He would end the period of silence by watching the noon devotional that a local pastor offered on the city's cable channel each day. Three weeks later, Harry called to cancel his second appointment for spiritual direction. "The miracle has come true!" he said. "I don't feel restless or dissatisfied most of the time, and when I do, it's a reminder to pay more attention to my body and to God's presence in the silence."

CONCLUSION: KEEPING FOCUSED

The practice of spiritual direction brings prayerful awareness to the presence of God in the life of (and for the sake of) another person. Like any conversation, however, the give-and-take dialogue of spiritual direction can become lost in a swamp of purposeless storytelling, sink into the quicksand of social chitchat, or bog down in the muck of human problems and limitations. Skillful spiritual directors can draw on the techniques and assumptions of brief psychotherapy and short-term pastoral counseling to keep the spiritual direction conversation from becoming mired in these unproductive exchanges. By focusing on daily life, tailoring care to the individual, identifying a directee's strengths and resources, and attending to possibilities, these directors turn the spiritual direction conversation toward the purposeful action that helps the directee become more aware of God's presence and to share greater intimacy with the Holy One who always seeks us out.

6

CONTEMPLATIVE ACTION: INTERVENTIONS FROM THE SPIRITUAL TRADITIONS

David cupped his hands around his coffee cup and looked his pastor in the eye. "Bottom line?" he asked. "Here's the bottom line—there's got to be more to relating to God than just going to worship, reading Scripture, and saying rote prayers." His tone was frustrated, even angry, and he blushed as he spoke.

Pastor Paul nodded. David and his wife, Mary, had been members of Paul's congregation for about two years; their three grade-school daughters were mainstays of the Sunday school program, but lately the family had missed worship two or three times a month. The third time Paul called to check on them, David asked to meet for coffee. Now his strong words about wanting "something more" spoke eloquently to Paul about the superficiality of much Christian worship and of the relationships among people in the congregation.

Both men took a sip of coffee, Paul nodding slightly. "There is more," he said after swallowing. "Much more. Not everyone wants it, but maybe you're one of those people God is calling to something different from treating church as a social club. Maybe you're called to a more passionate spirituality, a more immediate experience of God's presence, a stronger sense of the sacred that surrounds us every minute of every day." He stared directly into David's eyes as he spoke.

"Yes!" David exclaimed with gusto, eyes brightening. "That's what I'm after—passion and a sense of the holiness, the sacredness, of my everyday life. Worship just feels so dead, so routine. But if I don't get that sense of passion at church, how do I get it?"

The pastor chuckled. "I don't know exactly how *you'll* get it," he said. "I know how I get it. There are lots of ways it happens, and it's different for everybody. Here's what I can do for you. I can suggest some places to start looking. The Christian tradition—even our own denomination—

offers a lot of ways to reach out to God with passion, including prayer, spiritual disciplines, confession, and a lot more. What feeds you spiritually right now? What's one thing that makes you most passionate about God? Once you name it, we'll see if there's a Christian practice that seems to fit with it."

David is a lucky man. His pastor knows that as helpful as the skills and techniques of short-term psychotherapy might be to the practice of brief spiritual direction, secular approaches cannot replace the wisdom of the world's spiritual traditions. This practical, spiritual wisdom—shaped into (and distilled through) various spiritual disciplines and practices—has been honed through centuries of application in quiet desert hermitages, in the bustle and marketplaces of urban life, and in the midst of raising a family and earning a living. David may very well benefit from this wisdom, which could guide him to finding ways to bring more passion to his relationship with God.

This chapter draws on that spiritual wisdom to suggest some classic spiritual practices that work well in brief spiritual direction. These practices include introspection, contemplative awareness, sacred reading, confession, visualization, service to others, and developing a "rule of life." Discussion of these disciplines is necessarily limited here; entire books have been written about each of these practices. My intent is to suggest how some classic spiritual disciplines might enhance the process of brief spiritual direction, how the pastor or other spiritual guide might introduce them into the spiritual direction conversation, and how a director might follow up if a directee finds a particular practice helpful.

OPENING CONTEMPLATIVE SPACE

Many people who are frustrated by efforts to connect with God or to deepen prayer simply lack space in their life for contemplative awareness—that is, quiet reflection in the presence of God. If we imagine prayer as a language of intimacy through which God and humanity share their strongest and deepest connections, it is easy to see that each of us needs time and space in which to practice and master this special language. No friendship or marriage can endure unless the partners spend time together, sharing intimately of themselves and their experiences. Yet the speed, volume, pressures, and superficiality of many postmodern lives present significant hurdles to growing closer to other people, let alone to God.[1] The overall effect on spirituality is *loss of reverence*, an inability to stand in awe before the quiet power of God, to pay respect to the spiritual heart of life, and to speak fluently the language of prayer.

For this reason, often the first task in brief spiritual direction is to help people create space for contemplation in their lives—identifying the times and places in which intimate awareness of and communication with the holy are possible. Directors who note a lack of contemplative awareness in a person's life, or limited reverence in a directee, can practice "appropriate knowing" by drawing attention to this deficit. Contemplative awareness is, after all, a spiritual foundation for most of the world's religious traditions, and a director would be remiss not to mention this. If a directee, after a discussion of contemplative awareness and its importance to life with God, agrees that more space for contemplative awareness in his life might be fruitful, there are several ways to proceed.

The easiest way to begin is by identifying times in a person's life that provide opportunities for centering in the reality of God. Such times need not be long, nor steeped in solitude or silence. Myriad opportunities for contemplative awareness exist throughout a typical day. At each stoplight, for example, commuters can breathe deeply three times and recall that they are in the presence of God. When a mobile phone rings, its owner can breathe deeply before answering, letting the sound of the bell be a call to awareness of divine reality. (Zen master Thich Nhat Hanh suggests pausing when the phone rings to say, "Listen, listen: This beautiful sound calls me back to my true self.") Busy parents might repeat a one-word prayer, such as "Jesus," "love," or "peace," as a helpful way to center themselves as they prepare lunch, change diapers, or play with their children. Even the morning shower can be a contemplative space for a person who focuses on being cleansed to face the day as a child of the Lord.

Short prayers from the Celtic tradition can also be useful; for example, people could pray, "The same One that made thee made me likewise," each time they encounter someone in the hall at work. The Jesus Prayer—"Lord Jesus Christ, Son of God, have mercy on me," repeated in rhythm with the breath—is a classic spiritual discipline that can be taught and practiced in a few minutes.[2] A natural object—a stone, a flowering orchid, a weathered piece of driftwood—or a sacred symbol—an icon of Christ, a crucifix, or a Bible—can serve as an object of contemplation through which the directee seeks to see some aspect of divine reality. The point is to provide something on which the mind can focus, gradually developing an ability to concentrate on God in such a way as to exclude other, distracting thoughts, ideas, sights, and sounds.

In the conversation between David and Paul that opened this chapter, David told his pastor that he felt most passionate about God on his daily run. "Being on the trail at dusk, right in the middle of God's creation, feeling how powerful and active my body is, really connects me to the mystery of life," David said. Paul recommended using the time for running to open more contemplative space in David's life, suggesting that he begin to focus during the first half of the run on his gratitude for having a healthy body and on his awe at the complexity of his body's connections to the rest of creation—the ways in which his body takes in food, water, air, light and other gifts of the natural world. During the second half of the run, David was simply to listen in silence to see how God responded to his prayers of thanks and awe.

David found this approach helpful and soon shifted to mentally praying the word *thanks* each time his left foot hit the ground and the word *awe* each time his right foot hit the ground. After several weeks of this practice, he reported to Paul that he was feeling more in awe of God even when he wasn't running. Together, they worked at ways of expanding David's contemplative awareness to other parts of his day—his morning sales meeting, his weekend activities with his daughters, and times of lovemaking with Mary. As David began to bring this contemplative awareness to Sunday morning worship, he discovered in the liturgy a sense of the living Christ that he had never felt before.

In this example, David started opening contemplative space in the thirty to forty-five minutes of his daily run. Such a long period of contemplation would be ambitious for many people; in the beginning, most directees should aim to create just five to ten minutes of contemplative space in a busy life. Striving for longer periods of silence and reflection can frustrate people trying these disciplines for the first time. While longer periods are helpful, even a few minutes of reflection and centering can have a tremendous effect.

People new to contemplative awareness may find it helpful to experiment for several weeks, trying a variety of ways of creating contemplative space in their lives. Later, after they have some experience, they can settle on one or two approaches that seem most helpful to them. For example, using one-word prayers is rarely effective for me unless I use them in conjunction with a rosary, repeating my prayer word with each bead that passes through my fingers. Through experimentation, I have learned that combining a one-word prayer with a bodily action opens contemplative space for me more effectively than do simple verbal prayers or attention to the sights and sounds around me. Each of us has unique ways of creating contemplative space. Brief spiritual directors do well to encourage people to adapt traditional practices to their own needs or to invent new practices of their own.

LOOKING WITHIN

Ancient spiritual direction, especially as informed by the desert mothers and fathers, sought to alter a person's entire disposition—taking her ordinary (that is, sinful and self-centered) way of seeing, thinking, and acting and transforming it into the mind of Christ. Such transformation happens not all at once but through constant, tiny choices that alter a person in almost imperceptible ways, just as flowing water—given time—shapes solid rock into a channel for ever-flowing streams. Altering a person's disposition so that it escapes sin and cultural conditioning enough to see the world and other people through a prism of love is primarily a work of God's grace. But humans can participate in that process through a willingness to be transformed. During the patristic era of the church, a primary means of collaborating with such transformative work was the practice of *introspection*.

Introspection literally means "looking within." As used by the desert mothers and fathers, it carries the sense of *seeing clearly* and *honestly* who we are—identifying the best parts of ourselves and honestly naming the worst parts. "Introspection means looking inside ourselves to see what it is that makes us tick or fails to make us tick in order that we may love," writes church historian Roberta Bondi. "It has to do with observing ourselves to see what we think or feel or do that hurts us or makes us hurt others *so that we can do something about what needs to be corrected, and strengthen what needs to be strengthened.*"[3] In particular, introspection requires us to be honest about the passions—anger, fear, boredom, jealousy, sadness, joy—that prevent us from thinking, speaking, and acting with the mind of Christ. Introspection seeks to increase our freedom to choose actions consistent with our faith rather than ones that protect or enhance ourselves at the cost of other people or of honest, mutual relationships.

In brief spiritual direction, introspection can help people whose interactions with others (or whose internal reactions to the events of their lives) are consistently harmful or troubling. There are at least four ways introspection can be practiced in brief spiritual direction. First, directees who are focused on a particular event in their lives can be invited to imaginatively reenter the troubling experience in detail, feeling again the passions that were present in the moment. Those passions can be named aloud; once this happens, directors and directees can explore together how the passions influenced both the directees' behaviors and their awarenesses of God. The purpose of such exploration is to determine how directees might want to behave differently during similar circumstances in the future.

Second, directors can encourage people to practice "the disclosure of thoughts"—naming the types of thoughts, persistent or fleeting, that they notice taking hold of their consciousness. Disclosing these thoughts allows directees to discern honestly with the spiritual director whether their thoughts lead toward or away from God. Consciously naming the thoughts and speaking them aloud can change a directee's relationship to the passions behind the thoughts. This can allow directees to respond differently to the thoughts and passions the next time they occur.

Third, directors who perceive in a person's spiritual life the persistent presence of strong emotions or patterns of thought and behavior can ask permission to share their observations with the directee. Again, this practice makes the thoughts, behaviors, and passions conscious so that the directee might choose to relate differently to them. For example, when David expressed his frustration with worship, Pastor Paul might have said, "David, we've gotten to know each other pretty well over the past couple of years, and I think I see a pattern in your way of responding to God. It's a pattern that might keep prayer and worship from being passionate for you. I don't know if you want to hear about it, because it might be a difficult thing for you to hear. It might even make you feel ashamed.[4] What do you think? Do we have the sort of relationship where you could hear things like that from me?"

If David wanted to hear Paul's observations, the pastor could share his sense that David's concern with how others view him—which some people might call vanity—could keep him from being intimate with God and others. "I think vanity might keep you relating on a superficial level so you don't end up exposing anything negative about yourself," Paul might say. If David finds this observation helpful, the two could talk about the impact of vanity on David's life and how he would prefer to act when vanity becomes part of a conversation or relationship.

Fourth, people who want to look inside in order to increase their freedom to act in Christlike ways can seek feedback from others whom they trust. A spiritual director can suggest that a directee identify two or three people who can provide honest and valued feedback on patterns of thought or behavior that might impede the person's relationship with God and others. This feedback can then become fodder for future spiritual direction sessions (and for ongoing introspection) as the directee prays about the feedback and discerns how to respond in life-giving ways.

It is important that introspection of any type be followed by prayer— prayer for release from the unhelpful passions that dominate a person, prayers of gratitude for particular strengths or for increasing freedoms, and prayer for the transformation sought through introspection. In addition to praying, the spiritual director should—if the directee desires—hold the person accountable for changing patterns of thought or behavior that have been identified as troublesome through introspection. Making and acting on different choices in relationships and in ways of viewing the world takes practice; being held accountable for those choices in spiritual direction is one way of ensuring directees practice the changes they want to become.

CONFESSION

Frequently, people who initiate a spiritual direction conversation want to confess something that blocks their relationship with God and others. They are looking not for easy forgiveness or cheap grace but for someone to listen, to recognize the guilt or doubt they feel, and to affirm that God will accept them despite what they have said, thought, or done. At times, a ritual or act of penance negotiated between the director and directee can be helpful—for example, offering a gift to someone they have harmed or burning a letter in which they have listed their offenses. (It is important that the act or ritual be viewed not as a *means* of receiving forgiveness but as an opportunity to affirm and respond to both the seriousness of sin and the gift of graced forgiveness.) Both the Episcopal *Book of Common Prayer* and the Presbyterian *Book of Common Worship* offer liturgies for individual confession, which can be heard by laity in both traditions. In the Gospel of John, the risen Christ gave each Christian the authority both to hear a person's confession of sin and to forgive sin in the name of Jesus (John 20:23). Confession and forgiveness are vital aspects of Christian life.

In spiritual direction, confession is often addressed as the "manifestation" or "disclosure" of thoughts, as discussed in the previous section about introspection. In the disclosure of thoughts, directees reveal the thoughts (and the behaviors that resulted from those thoughts) that led them away from God. This exercise can provide both accountability and the experience of forgiveness.[5] In fact, historically there has been an overlap between spiritual direction as "the disclosure of thoughts" and the Roman Catholic sacrament of confession. In both confession and spiritual direction, "it is essential that the story be told candidly, that sins and shortcomings be named, and that . . . directee[s] see [themselves] clearly."[6]

One way of receiving a confession, as suggested by Quaker theologian Richard Foster, is for the director and directee to pray together, inviting

God to reveal anything in the directee's life for which he or she needs forgiveness or healing (or both).[7] After a period of silence, the directee names aloud those things that God has revealed. Once the confession has been made, the director and directee again sit in silence; the director ends the silence with words of assurance that God has forgiven the directee. Then the director prays, giving thanks for God's grace and asking for continued healing and wholeness in the directee's life. Foster reminds us that it is especially important to pray for the healing of the directee's inner wounds caused by sin.[8]

After confession, it is appropriate and important for the director and directee to talk about how the directee will avoid the sin confessed—and others like it—in the future. Visualizing a situation in which temptation might occur and practicing a different, preferred response can help a directee feel prepared to encounter a difficult circumstance again. Such rehearsal can also assure the directee that a change of heart has occurred as a result of her confession, that she has been not only forgiven but also renewed in important ways.

SPIRITUAL READING

Attending to God's Word through the reading and study of Scripture is a mainstay of Christian spirituality. Sometimes, however, people become so mesmerized by the historical and sociocultural contexts of Scripture, or by efforts to identify the "meaning" of a particular passage, that they forget to read Scripture prayerfully and imaginatively. When this happens, people may experience Scripture as dry and static; the Bible ceases to be God's living word to them and to their communities.

The prayer practice of "divine reading," or *lectio divina*, can be one way of offsetting this tendency. Divine reading helps people approach Scripture from a more contemplative stance and, once they have actively reflected on the Word, to enter into dialogue with God about what they have encountered in their reading. The four steps of this discipline—reading, meditating, speaking, and listening—can be taught and practiced in a single session of brief spiritual direction, after which directees who find divine reading helpful can practice it on their own. Whether practiced at home or during a spiritual direction conversation, however, the prayerful dialogue that emerges and evolves from divine reading can provide important material for directors and directees to process during future spiritual direction meetings.

The first step of divine reading is to read slowly a biblical passage or other short text aloud, listening with an open heart. It can help for someone other than the directee to read the text so that the person entering into the prayer of divine reading need only listen. Listening is done from a particular stance, however; the person praying attends to the reading with his or her awareness attuned to whether particular words or phrases seem to catch the attention or call forth emotions. Sometimes this type of listening becomes easier if the selected text is read aloud several times with silent pauses between readings.

The second step is meditation on the text. In this stage of divine reading, the person actively meditates on what has been heard. God's Word is welcomed into the heart so that a person's entire being can be illumined by the text's message. Directees can imagine themselves as characters in the biblical story they have heard, for example, seeing Zacchaeus in the tree and hearing Jesus call out to him, or smelling the dust as the disciples trod the road to Emmaus. While imagining themselves in the scene, directees attend to their emotional and physical reactions to the events of the text. Alternatively, directees might also "think through" a particular text, looking at their own situations through the lens of the passage, discursively thinking about its meanings and its application to their lives. Using commentaries to identify historical and cultural influences on the text can be helpful in this step, as long as this activity does not interfere with the contemplative process.

In the third step, directees speak from the heart about their meditations on the text. This stage initiates a dialogue with Christ about what has been heard, experienced, and learned from the biblical passage. It is an active rather than a receptive stage; directees can pray aloud or use words internally to express their understanding of what God has been saying to them through the passage read. In this stage, directees might also commit to a particular action they feel is an appropriate response to what they have heard. Such a commitment may be offered tentatively, with a prayer asking God to confirm whether the response is appropriate.

In the final step of divine reading, directees listen receptively in silence for God's response to their spoken prayers. While listening, directees attend to inner movements of the spirit—feelings of joy or sorrow, spontaneous tears, or perhaps even a spoken word from the Holy Spirit. As directees contemplate on the reading, their meditation, and their spoken prayer, they seek to open their hearts to intuitive or "illogical" insights about their lives. The time of silent listening might be ended by a simple "Amen" or a more formal prayer of response.

Divine reading can create a powerful context in which directees may experience God's presence and action. Whatever response is heard during the listening stage can become the subject of the spiritual direction conversation, as director and directee discern together an appropriate response to God's work during the practice of divine reading.

RULE OF LIFE

Developing a "rule of life"—a formal list of ways to attend to the rhythms and facets of one's spiritual and religious life and relationships—is a classic tool in spiritual direction. Borrowed from the monastic tradition, a rule of life spells out the activities that nourish a person's spirit and help the person tend to relationships with God and creation. "Making explicit the rule by which our lives are implicitly lived," writes spiritual director Joseph Driskill, "provides an opportunity to reflect upon and shape the ways we nurture our spirits. Making a Rule of Life simply involves listing the things we do to nurture our spirit."[9] Everything a person does to nourish the spirit should be included on the list— including, for example, worshipping with a congregation, walking on the beach, praying in the morning, giving and receiving massage, reading Scripture, dancing, singing, and fasting.

Once a rule of life has been set forth in writing, the directee can consciously add or subtract items to ensure a "balanced diet" in her spiritual life. She then commits to making a priority of the activities included in the rule of life. While the term *rule of life* sounds stern, this tool is not intended as a list of legalistic do's and don'ts. Rather, a rule of life is a guideline for structuring life in ways that allow a person to receive life and grace by attending to the many aspects of her spiritual life and being.

If directors sense that a rule of life would benefit a directee, they can tentatively suggest its use by first explaining what a rule is and how it works. Again, it is an example of "appropriate knowing" for a spiritual director to speak of a rule of life as a useful part of the Christian traditions of spiritual discipline. But the subject is best introduced from a not-knowing stance that communicates the directee's freedom to reject the suggestion. The director might say, for example, "I'm not certain this would be helpful in your case, but many people of faith find it useful to develop a daily, weekly, monthly, and annual rhythm for the ways in which they attend to God's presence. It's usually called a 'rule of life.' Would you like to learn more about it and see if it feels right for you?" Once the concept has been explained, directors can see whether the person is interested in developing a personal rule of life.

Helping people to identify the rhythms of their spiritual lives and to build those rhythms into a consistent routine is an ongoing process that can be initiated in one or two meetings. Some people find it transforming to look at the ways they spend their time and invest their identities as signs pointing to what is spiritually important to them. Almost all people who seek spiritual direction are at some level "concerned with . . . the stewardship of their time and energy (as well as their substance) and are looking for help in shaping their days."[10] Margaret Guenther suggests that a rule of life be structured around four relationship patterns: to God, to others, to creation, and to self.[11] Above, I suggested that people identify the daily, weekly, monthly, and annual activities that give substance to their spiritual lives.

Pastor Paul, in the earlier example, might point out to David that his informal rule of life already includes a daily run in a contemplative state of mind, weekly worship in community, weekly playtime with his daughters, and monthly celebration of the Lord's Supper with the congregation. These activities focus primarily on David's relationships to God and to others. A more formal rule of life for David might flesh out the activities through which he intends to relate to self and to creation—through monthly "quiet days" spent fishing alone, for example, or an annual retreat with the family to help build a house in Mexico.

Once a rule of life has been developed, a spiritual director can help hold people accountable for attending to the activities it includes. In general, it is good practice to review and revise a personal rule of life annually or during any major life change, such as the birth of a child or the beginning of a new job. The routines and activities included in a rule of life should be flexible, able to be adjusted to the changing demands a person's life makes on limited time and resources. (Some people, however, constantly amend their rules of life in ways that allow them to avoid spiritual commitments. In such cases, a spiritual director might "nudge" people to attend to whatever dynamics keep them from nurturing their relationship with God in the intentional way they had hoped when they wrote their rules of life.)

VISUALIZATION

Visualizing new ways of responding to temptation, mentally rehearsing different choices in a difficult situation, or projecting oneself into a biblical story through imagination can be powerful interventions in spiritual direction. Indeed, visualization has a rich history in the Christian traditions as a way of encountering God in prayer, coming to a deeper understanding of Scripture, and incorporating personally meaningful symbols and images from dreams into a person's spiritual life. Much in the Ignatian approach to the discernment of God's will (see chapter 7) relies on imagination and visualization. I especially find imagination and visualization helpful in spiritual direction with people who learn visually, experience God communicating with them through dreams, or respond viscerally to art and images.

Visualization can be particularly helpful for breaking free of spiritual ruts or dryness in prayer, which are sometimes caused by a rational, linear approach to spirituality. The following visualization, based on an Ignatian spiritual exercise, can help when people feel "stuck" in their relationship with God or are seeking God's guidance to understand the next step they are called to take in their lives. For example, I used this visualization with a woman who was trying to discern how God wanted her to interact with the employees of her company. We started with some breathing exercises that allowed her to relax and focus her attention inward. Then I slowly read the following:

> You are standing outside a door. Notice its material and shape. Inside is a statue made to commemorate your life. Feel your emotions as you reach for the door and step inside.
>
> Stand at the doorway and look at the statue in the center of the room. Notice its shape, its material. Notice the colors, the mood, the size. Now walk closer. Walk all around the statue, noticing its detail. Touch it. Feel the texture, the temperature, and the materials it is made of.

The directee saw a statue of herself as "the intrepid leader," bravely setting a course while her employees lined up to follow single file behind her. She stood on a rock above the others, pointing into the distance. The visualization continued:

> Now you become aware of another presence in the room. Jesus has entered and is watching you from the doorway. You step back and watch him walk all around the statue of your life, noticing it. He is intensely curious about the statue. Watch Jesus interact with it. What emotions does it raise in you as you watch him?
>
> Now Jesus reaches out to touch the statue. He changes it in some way, making an adjustment to this record of your life. Then he leaves.
>
> Approach the statue again. Walk around it as before and take note of the change that Jesus made. Notice your thoughts and feelings as you walk around this new statue.

Now you will take leave of the statue. You make some action
to honor this work of art. Then you walk back through the
door. You may open your eyes whenever you feel ready.

Jesus rearranged the woman's statue so that she and her employees
were standing in a circle on even ground, consulting a map as the
woman's face communicated support and concern—an approach she
named "leading alongside," which became a metaphor for understanding how God related to her on her own journey.

Whenever I use this meditation in spiritual direction, the changes
Jesus makes to directees' statues provide rich, powerful material for spiritual direction. The changes serve to move directees from a stuck position to more active collaboration with God's intentions for their lives.

SERVING OTHERS

The tradition of Christian spiritual theology has always emphasized that
spiritual disciplines are undertaken, and spiritual growth occurs, so that
people can be strengthened and transformed to act in the world with
compassion. One eucharistic liturgy prays, "Draw us, O God, to your
heart at the heart of the world"; and this is ultimately the prayer of all
who seek to know and love God.[12] Serving others in the name of God as
a spiritual discipline is the practice of reconciliation in action; it serves to
mend the broken pieces of creation as people act as "little Christs" to one
another and to the entire cosmos. Through service in the world, we share
with others the source of life we have tapped through the practice of
spiritual disciplines and open ourselves to knowing God in a new way
through service.

In brief spiritual direction, a pastor or other spiritual guide might
quickly discern that particular people have "spiritualized" their relationships with God to such an extent that they disdain or ignore the material world. Others never experience God in or through other people;
indeed, they may only recognize interior experiences of God. Others
may come to spiritual direction feeling puzzled by a seemingly "non-
spiritual" call to engage with the world in particular ways—for example,
volunteering at an AIDS hospice, creating a compost pile for a community garden, or transforming a railroad right-of-way into a bicycle trail.

All of these people might be well served by a spiritual director who
suggests they begin volunteer service in the community as an expression
of their spirituality. (In fact, Baron von Hugel, a famous British spiritual
director of the early twentieth century, insisted that his most precocious

directee volunteer in a soup kitchen if she wanted to remain in a spiritual direction relationship with him!)

Like the practice of divine reading, service to others can create the conditions through which a person can experience God's action and presence amid daily life. Volunteer activities should be chosen to reflect the gifts and interests of the directee. But people not only should do those things for which they have a particular aptitude or interest but should also have a sense of "call" to a particular activity, a feeling that God is inviting the person to participate in the work of reconciliation through this form of service.

In many ways, the process of discerning whether one is called to a particular form of service to others is much like divine reading—the person senses an inner tug or a quickening of the heart and then reflects and meditates on that call, prays about it as honestly as possible, and listens in silence for God's response. Brief spiritual direction can focus both on the process of discerning a call to a particular form of service and on the effects such service has on an individual's relationship with God and others.

CONCLUSION: KNOWING HOW AND WHY SPIRITUAL DISCIPLINES ARE APPROPRIATE

Many other spiritual disciplines can be adapted for use in brief spiritual direction, and individual directors will have favorite practices or be aware of Jewish, Buddhist, Hindu, or Muslim disciplines that seem suitable for a particular directee. No matter what tradition such disciplines are drawn from, however, it is important that they be chosen with a mind to sharpening a person's awareness of God's presence and action in the world. They should not be presented as a means to obtaining "exotic" spiritual experience or to glorifying the person who practices them. In addition, directors should avoid recommending or teaching spiritual disciplines that they have not practiced themselves; it is difficult to guide others when one has not experienced the terrain personally.

It is also important in brief spiritual direction that interventions from the spiritual traditions be chosen for their capacity to create new (or at least different) opportunities for a person to be in dialogue with God. After all, brief spiritual direction emphasizes reflection on God's presence and action and discernment of an appropriate response to God's work in a person's life; spiritual guides should suggest spiritual exercises that enhance, not detract from, this dual focus. Finally, spiritual exercises suggested during brief spiritual direction should not be practiced in a vacuum—that is, introduced to directees and never discussed again. Especially in the beginning stages of practicing a particular discipline, directees must take time to debrief their experiences with a director who is intimately familiar with that discipline.

7

THE ART OF DISCERNMENT
IN BRIEF SPIRITUAL DIRECTION

Tom Pham looked at the anxious faces of the couple seated on the couch across from him. For two weeks in a row, Ron and Tina Krauter had visited Saturday night worship at Covenant Church, and after the second visit Pastor Tom called to ask if they would like to have a cup of coffee. Ron eagerly accepted, inviting the minister to the couple's house the very next day.

For nearly an hour, the pastor listened to the aging couple sadly explain their growing discomfort with Old First Church, the congregation where both had been baptized and where Ron's parents and grandparents had been members for decades. The doctrine and liturgy of the church felt confining to them; in recent years, the congregation seemed to them more concerned with maintaining a historically ethnic identity than with addressing the immediate concerns of parishioners—especially the concerns of a newly married retired couple with six grown children. Tina was frustrated and confused by the authoritarian and sexist attitudes of the congregation's pastor. For months the couple had secretly visited churches from other denominations; now they were on the verge of making a decision about leaving Old First.

"We really feel at home at your church," Ron said. "We don't know everything your denomination believes, and sometimes worship seems a little informal, but we really feel drawn to your church."

Tina nodded and smiled, but tears in her eyes signaled the turmoil of her heart.

"We feel ready to make a change in church membership," she said, dabbing at her eyes with a tissue. "But one thing bothers us, Pastor Pham. How do we know God wants us to leave Old First and become members at Covenant Church? How do we know this is the right thing to do, something God wants, and not just something we're choosing out of our own sinfulness?"

The Krauters are asking Pastor Tom for help with *discernment*—clarifying God's will in relation to a specific decision. Discernment, sometimes called "the discernment of spirits," has been characterized as a "means to sift through, distinguish, separate, and divide interior movements that result from God's personal involvement" in people's lives.[1] In many ways, the practice of spiritual direction can be considered primarily a ministry of discernment; in spiritual direction, as emphasized throughout this text, directors and directees listen together for God's presence and movement in a person's life, then choose a response appropriate to God's self-communication. The overarching goal of spiritual direction is to help people make choices and take action congruent with God's hopes for their lives at a particular time.[2]

It is not unusual for people who seek brief spiritual direction to do so out of a concern for a particular choice they must make—about a job or a relationship, the way to use their money and other resources, the possibility of moving to a new city, or the wisdom of attending graduate school. The perspectives of pastors and other spiritual guides have value as people seek to choose the path that best parallels the desires of God.

Fortunately, Christian traditions of spirituality offer significant resources for the spiritual director who is leading others in a discernment process. It is important to understand that discernment is a prayerful activity involving both reason and imagination; the process is not scientific but, as David Duncombe has said, "mostly . . . intuitive." It is "similar to the experience of recognizing a childhood friend years later, in a way that seems uncanny. Everything about him or her has changed; not even the most complete FBI description would have enabled us to recognize this person, yet we do."[3] Recognizing God's will occurs through a sort of "heart knowledge" in which a truth is grasped with all of one's being, whether it gradually comes into focus over time or strikes instantly in a flash of insight.

This intuitive recognition of God's desire for (or call in) a person's life can occur in brief spiritual direction by drawing on principles of Christian discernment developed by the desert mothers and fathers in the second century. These early guidelines for understanding God's desire were refined in the sixteenth century by Ignatius Loyola, founder of the Jesuit order, who interpreted and applied the guidelines in a somewhat systemized way. Recognizing that the process of discernment can be complex and confusing, I describe here a simple approach to clarifying God's will in ways appropriate to short-term spiritual direction. My approach is based in large part on the Ignatian principles for discernment set forth in the classic text *Spiritual Exercises*, which I have reimagined through the lens of brief pastoral counseling described in chapter 3.

MOVEMENTS OF THE SOUL AND NORMS FOR DISCERNMENT

In general, spiritual theology identifies three movements of the soul that the spiritual director might encounter in the process of discernment: (1) positive and life-giving instincts born of prayer, which are carefully and accurately interpreted and then used as a basis of action; (2) negative and harmful instincts rooted in idolatry, selfish impulses, or sinful distortions of God's presence and activity, which are acted on without proper or accurate interpretation; and (3) human choices not overtly influenced by prayer but rooted in an accurate experience and understanding of church doctrine and spiritual realities.[4] Discernment requires a person to accurately identify the type of soul movement being experienced and to interpret it carefully so that her choice can be measured against the standard of God's desires for that person and for all of creation. It is important to note that movements of the soul come about through God's personal involvement with a person; movements of the soul are not independent of a person's relationship with God.[5]

The practice of discernment in the Christian tradition assumes that God's desires for a specific situation are revealed in prayer. Scripture, tradition, and reason all contribute to the discernment process, but ultimate success requires an active dialogue in prayer between God and the person seeking clarity about a choice or action. Because discernment occurs through prayerful dialogue between a person and God, responsibility for discernment (and for the choices that follow) rests with the person seeking guidance, not with the spiritual director. Nonetheless, a director can assist with the process of discernment, suggesting specific ways to listen for God's will and weighing the directee's insights against traditional norms for discernment.

Norms and criteria by which to judge the outcome of discernment have evolved throughout the centuries, and they continue to shift as we gain more understanding of human behavior and the distortions of experience created by systemic sin. Nonetheless, a broad consensus exists about appropriate criteria for making a human decision that is congruent with God's wishes. Some norms and criteria for assessing the results of discernment, as identified by English spiritual theologian Martin Thornton, include the following:[6]

- God's will in a given situation might be mysterious, confusing, or puzzling, but it will not be irrational or futile. A sense of despair or hopelessness in discernment, or a choice that leads to an action that cannot be accomplished, suggests that God's will has not been accurately discerned.

- God desires people to act morally, and godly courses of action benefit, not harm, the individuals and communities to whom an individual relates. Note that God's will is not revealed solely for the benefit of the person seeking discernment, but for all of creation. Decisions arrived at through discernment should be consistent with God's will revealed in Christ and witnessed to by Scripture.

- Being in touch with God's will for a specific situation brings a sense of inner peace, in which a person remains humble and unattached to specific outcomes. Rather than being anxious or striving for a particular result, people who have accurately discerned God's call abandon themselves to God's intentions without concern for outcome.

- A genuine prompting of the Spirit creates flexibility rather than rigidity. As stated above, people who clearly understand God's wishes will not be attached to or insist on a particular outcome for their actions. Rather, such people are buoyed by a peaceful desire to act in ways that please God, no matter what the consequences might be.

KEYS TO DISCERNMENT: CONSOLATION AND DESOLATION

Emotions—especially the feelings that bubble up and pass away (or occasionally take up semipermanent residence) during and after prayer—are central to the process of discernment described by Ignatius. He believed that peace, joy, anxiety, anger, frustration, and other emotions point toward God's movement in the soul. Likewise, he believed emotions also point to the soul's movements toward and away from God. In broad terms, Ignatius spoke and wrote about two types of emotional movement in the soul: moments of *consolation*, when a person's heart and will are aligned with God and bring a sense of peace and interior freedom; and moments of *desolation*, when God feels far away and the heart and will are caught in a person's own desires, curtailing freedom and leading to anxious, compulsive, and egotistical behaviors.[7] Being able to identify moments of consolation and moments of desolation is an essential skill for discernment.

A person's thoughts and emotions during and after prayer are central to distinguishing consolation from desolation. "Consolation," Maureen Conroy writes, "results in encouraging thoughts; desolation causes discouraging thoughts."[8] Experiences that bring immediate encouragement and joy, however, may later cause anxiety and discouragement. These are considered "false consolations." The possibility of false consolation clarifies why a person should be wary of acting immediately on a movement of the soul that seems to be consoling. No matter how clear an emotional response to a movement of the soul may seem, over time subtle (or not-so-subtle) variations can appear. Emotional responses that are consistent and persistent over time can be most trusted for making decisions and taking action congruent with God's wishes.

In general, experiences of desolation—anxiety, emptiness, unrest, and spiritual discomfort—are explicit evidence that an experience, decision, or action is not congruent with God's will. This does not mean, however, that experiences of consolation will be free of anxiety. Understanding God's wishes can cause a person to worry or be anxious, but such feelings are not a result of God's involvement. Rather, they reflect the presence of sin or "the enemy" distorting the person's response. Beneath these feelings of disturbance will be a deep sense of peace—an intuitive recognition that God's intentions are clear. Such peace never exists when God acts to create desolation in the soul.

Distinguishing between true and false consolation requires the spiritual guide to inquire carefully into the precise thoughts and emotions that surround a person's decisions and to listen carefully to how those thoughts and emotions are described. Pastor Tom Pham, for example, responded to Tina Krauter's tearful worries about changing churches by saying, "The thought of leaving Old First seems upsetting to you. Tell me about the thoughts and feelings you've had as you've tried to decide whether to join another church."

"Well," Tina said, her tears immediately stopping, "when we first started visiting other churches, we both had a sense of excitement, a sense of new possibility. And as we kept worshipping in other places, both of us had a peaceful feeling that we haven't had about Old First in a long time. I'd always had faith and felt love, but it was the first time I felt hopeful about church. That hope brings such a sense of peace."

Ron nodded in agreement. "She's right. She felt it first, but that sense of peace made me feel like it was OK to keep visiting other churches. And when we got to Covenant Church, I had an immediate sense of 'coming home.' Your place just felt right to me, and Tina said she felt it too."

Listening to their comments, Pastor Tom felt reasonably certain that Ron and Tina had experienced consolation. But he wasn't yet clear whether that consolation was true or false. "Ron," he asked, "is the thought of leaving Old First as upsetting for you as it is for Tina?"

"Not at all," Ron said immediately. "I mean, I know my grandma and my mom are going to roll over in their graves—and I feel guilty about that—but I feel like I'm leaving a foreign country and going to the place God wants me to be. It's like I've slipped the right key into the lock for the first time in my life."

Tom nodded. Ron's response suggested an experience of true consolation. "Tina," the pastor asked, "when did the worrying start for you?"

"I just feel scared whenever I think about moving my membership," she said. "I start to feel like maybe I'm not hearing God correctly, maybe I'm confusing my will with God's will. It's confusing and upsetting—but when I take a deep breath and ask for God's guidance, I still feel that sense of peace, that sense of coming home. I know it's right, even though I have doubts."

Tom smiled. Tina's words suggested that her experience wasn't false consolation but "the enemy" seeking to confuse her and lead her away from God's guidance.

"I think you should trust that peaceful feeling right now," Tom told the couple. "Offer your decision to God, and see if you still feel as peaceful about it, or even more peaceful, in a few days or few weeks. Take your time. You'll know when the time is right to make a decision."

Ron looked at Tina. "Honestly, Pastor," he said, "it feels like the decision's been made. Right now we're just trying to get comfortable with it." Tina nodded.

Experiences of desolation are sometimes confused with depression. Clinical depression is quite different from spiritual desolation or the radical experience of "the dark night of the soul" (although the experiences are often conflated in the literature of pastoral care and counseling). A director's love for the person seeking guidance, as well as guidelines for the ethical practice of ministry, requires careful inquiry about experiences of desolation in order to clarify whether a person ought to be assessed for depression by a qualified medical professional.

In general, desolation and experiences of the dark night may include a sense of God's absence, loss of faith or certainty of belief, a sense of aimless spiritual wandering without an anchor point, and deep sorrow about the ways in which one has failed God. In these ways, spiritual desolation may be similar to depression. However, unlike depression, desolation and the dark night of the soul do not usually cause a person to function poorly at work, at home, or in relationships; a person's mood is not unusually marked by irritability; and the person rarely pleads for help but has a sense that the desolation is an important experience.[9] Depression, on the other hand, is usually marked by a variety of symptoms that persist for two weeks or more, including irritability, a sense of hopelessness or sadness, tearfulness, suicidal thoughts, disruptions in sleeping or eating patterns, weight loss or gain, and a loss of effectiveness in daily life. If a spiritual director suspects that a person might be suffering from clinical depression instead of (or caused by) spiritual desolation, he should direct the person to seek medical assessment to rule out illness that could invalidate the process of discernment.

GETTING STARTED

In brief spiritual direction, a clear and specific question is necessary before embarking on the process of discernment. Establishing the question for which an answer is being discerned is similar to identifying a goal for the spiritual direction conversation. In clarifying the question, it can help for the director to ask questions that help the directee make the question as specific, time limited, and action oriented as possible. For example, Tina Krauter presented Pastor Tom Pham with a clear and specific question for discernment: Does God want us to transfer our membership from Old First Church to Covenant Church? The question is a good one for discernment because it identifies both a specific decision (leaving Old First) and a specific action (transferring to Covenant Church) for which God's will is being sought. Pastor Tom could sharpen or clarify the question further by including a time frame: Does God want the Krauters to transfer their membership from Old First Church to Covenant Church *now*?

If someone asks for discernment of a broad, vague, or general question (for example, "What does God want me to do with my life?" or "How does God want me to treat other people?"), the spiritual director will need to spend some time clarifying what the person wants to know. Helpful questions for clarifying an issue for discernment include the following:

- What options or choices are you trying to choose between?
- What part of your life—work, relationships, finances, living arrangements—are you trying to clarify?
- What is the first question that needs to be answered in order for you to take a small step toward making a choice or decision?
- What piece of information, if it were clarified, would make the biggest difference to you right now in terms of being prepared to take action?

Often, questions for discernment are best posed as a specific action the person is considering—not, for example, "Am I being called to ministry?" but "Should I begin exploring whether to attend seminary?" or "Is it time to ask my pastor about the ordination process for my denomination?"

With a clear question in mind, the spiritual director can assess what sort of discernment process might help most. To do so, the director must ask: "Do you already sense God's call in this situation, or does God seem entirely silent?" and "If you do sense God's call or will, is the answer clear or still uncertain?" The directee's answers will suggest which of the "discernment times" identified by Ignatius is at play in the process.

GAINING CLARITY DURING "REASONING TIME"

Ignatius describes three "times" in which discernment takes place. The first—"revelation time"—is relatively rare. At such a time, God's call or desire is absolutely clear; a person understands without a doubt what action or decision is right. More common is "reasoning time"—instances in which a person is not sure what God desires or in which God's voice has not been (or cannot be) heard, and a decision or action must be reasoned through. (The term *reason*, however, means not only rational thought but also imagination.) The third time for discernment—which is somewhat awkwardly called the "second time"—is a period of confirming God's desire. The second time is a period of verifying that God's position on the issue has been clearly discerned. Directees enter into second time once a decision has been made through revelation or reasoning.

Most discernment in brief spiritual direction will occur in reasoning time. (People in revelation time rarely seek help with discernment until they have entered second time.) In reasoning time, four approaches or techniques can help the director and directee. The first draws on the rational faculty of logic; the other three rely on imagination and visualization. All stimulate experiences of consolation or desolation, which can then be explored in the spiritual direction conversation.

The first approach is simply to weigh the pros and cons of a specific choice—a rational cost/benefit analysis. "If you did transfer your membership to Covenant Church," Pastor Tom might ask the Krauters, "what would the benefits be? What would be the drawbacks?" It helps to list the costs and benefits side by side in two columns on a piece of paper or on a whiteboard so they can be seen together. After the directee has exhausted the options in each column, the director can ask whether the benefits of a particular decision outweigh the costs. Careful attention should be directed to the thoughts and emotions that surface in the directee during this process; the initial movements of the soul toward consolation or desolation should be noted.

At times, a logical, linear investigation of the costs and benefits of a particular decision is all that is needed to clarify a directee's choice.

Sometimes, however, this process further confuses the issue, and no clear experience of desolation and consolation occurs (or there may be competing experiences of these movements of the soul). In such a case, the director can turn to three imaginative exercises.

USING IMAGINATIVE EXERCISES FOR DISCERNMENT

Before beginning these exercises, directees may find it helpful to close their eyes and breathe deeply until they are relaxed. Distractions in the room—noise, light, the presence of other people—should be minimized. After a time of silence, the director may choose to pray that God's presence, protection, and guidance will be with the directee during the visualization. When the directee is relaxed and ready to begin, the director offers one or more of the following scenarios:

Imagine a friend comes to see you about a choice she has to make. Picture her clearly in your mind. [*Pause.*] Feel yourself being present to her and willing to listen carefully to the issues she is struggling to resolve. You ask her what choice she is wrestling with, and you are surprised to discover it is the same question you are asking. Now, in your mind, ask her the questions you think are pertinent to consider, and listen with a discerning heart to her answers. When you are done asking questions and listening to answers, nod your head or raise your hand. [*Pause until the directee indicates the period of questioning and answering has ended.*] Now your friend looks you in the eye and asks sincerely what she ought to do. What will you tell her? Speak it aloud now. [*Pause.*] When you are ready to talk about what you have learned, open your eyes slowly and stretch, feeling the energy flow through your body. I will stay quiet until you speak.

Imagine you are lying in your bed. You will die in a few hours. Picture the details of the room you are in. [*Pause.*] If you do not want to die alone, imagine the people who will be around you. Picture their faces, their clothes, the ways they look at you, the things they say. [*Pause.*] Knowing that your body will die soon, you begin to review the events of your life. [*Pause.*] Soon you consider the decision you are weighing today. On your deathbed, imagine the impact of every choice you could have made about this issue. [*Pause.*] As you lie dying, which choice do you wish you had made? When you are ready to talk about what you have learned, open your eyes slowly and stretch, feeling the energy flow through your body. I will stay quiet until you speak. [*Pause until the directee is ready to talk about the visualization.*]

Imagine that Christ has returned or that you have died, and you are standing before him for judgment. Picture his face as he looks at you. Feel the emotions and thoughts that course through your awareness. [*Pause.*] Imagine that Jesus begins to mentally review your life on earth, considering each significant choice you have made in life. Notice the look on his face, the sense of energy he directs your way. [*Pause.*] Somehow, you are aware that he is now reviewing the choice you are trying to discern today. He looks at you with compassion, weighing the faithfulness of your decision. At this moment, as you watch him judge the choice you are making today, what decision do you wish you had made? Let that wish permeate your consciousness. Notice the emotions and images that you experience as you are aware of what choice you wish Jesus were considering right now. [*Pause.*] When you are ready to talk about what you have learned, open your eyes slowly and stretch, feeling the energy flow through your body. I will stay quiet until you speak. [*Pause until the directee is ready to talk about the visualization.*]

When the directee is ready to talk about the visualization, the director asks about the predominant thoughts and emotions that surfaced during the exercise, attending carefully to the words and metaphors the directee uses. Questions should focus on clarifying whether the experience was primarily one of consolation or one of desolation. When the conversation seems to have ended, the director may want to ask if the directee would like to say anything more. If not, the director may gently inquire, "Is your choice any clearer now than when we first began talking?"

OFFERING A DECISION TO GOD

Discernment is not complete even after a directee has a clearer idea of God's wishes. Rather, the discernment process now moves into second time, with the directee seeking God's acceptance of the decision or confirmation of the discernment process. To initiate the second time of discernment, the directee offers the decision to God in prayer, specifically asking for clarity about whether the discernment process has accurately understood God's desire and correctly interpreted the indications of consolation. For a few days—or longer, if necessary—the directee should pause for a few moments each day to listen in silence for God's response, attending to the movements of the soul that emerge as the decision or action is held before God. If consolation continues to be the primary affective response, the directee may thank God for participating in the discernment process and move forward in faith. If desolation surfaces and persists, further discernment may be necessary.

CONCLUSION: REMAINING TENTATIVE

With rare exceptions, no discernment process can bring absolute satisfaction that God's desire for a person's life has been accurately understood. Humans are embedded in sin that warps our perceptions; this sin also twists our desire to participate in God's ongoing acts of creation, which seek to bring the cosmos to the wholeness guaranteed in Christ. No matter how carefully we listen for God's call, we always act in faith, without absolute assurance that what we are doing is finally in accordance with God's purposes. (It is worth remembering that some of humanity's most appalling actions have been—and are—committed in God's name.) But if a discernment process is entered into with intention, a directee can feel confident that God's guidance has been sought and faithfully considered—and that grace will be extended if God's call has been misunderstood, distorted as we have acted on it despite our initial understanding, or even willfully ignored. God is good, no matter what.

8

SPIRITUAL GUIDANCE
WITH COUPLES AND FAMILIES

Most spiritual guidance focuses on the relationship between God and an individual, but God also relates to families. Pastors—both because of their proximity to families as a whole and because of their individual relationships with the different generations of a single family—are in a unique position to help families with their corporate spiritual lives. While families typically seek a pastor's guidance for interpersonal difficulties, an alert pastor will also attend to their spiritual condition. This is especially important because research suggests that couples and families with a strong, shared spiritual life are healthier and better able to weather the inevitable strains of postmodern culture.

A number of studies correlate family wellness and marital satisfaction with religious/spiritual belief and practice. These studies also suggest, however, that simple participation in religious activities and attendance in worship may not result in a stronger marriage. Rather, as Paul Giblin notes, "spirituality *to the degree that it is an integral part of the relationship*, influencing communication, conflict-resolution, decision-making, and sexuality, among other dimensions, likely results in increased relationship-satisfaction."[1] A spirituality woven into the daily lives and values of a family—talked about when the children are disciplined, included in the breakfast conversation, allowed to influence budgeting decisions, present at times of play—promises to have a greater impact on family members and their relationships than either a spirituality that remains isolated and fragmented (the possession of individuals) or a spirituality that is limited to a specific time and place, such as Sunday worship.

Yet most family therapists and other counselors lack the training to work with a couple's or family's spirituality as an integral part of the relationship. These professionals perform important work, but often they do not have a theological foundation, and sometimes they do not have an experience of deeply lived faith, to inform their work with families and couples. Such professionals must rely on the family or the couple to guide them in relation to spirituality rather than serving as guides themselves. Thus, clergy—who usually have theological training and spiritual depth in addition to remarkable access to families—must be ready to integrate spirituality into their care of couples and families. This chapter suggests ways pastors can draw on the resources of Christian spirituality and the discipline of family counseling as they work with families.

WHAT IS FAMILY "SPIRITUALITY"?

In this chapter, the term *spirituality* refers both to the relationship between God and a family as a whole and to the relationships between God and the individual members of a family. All of these relationships with God— communal and individual—have concrete effects on a family's life because they involve family members in behavioral responses to God.[2] Paying attention to a family's behavioral responses to God is a key to providing effective short-term spiritual direction to couples and families in the parish. As with individuals, spiritual direction with families and couples centers on identifying how God is at work in the family and discerning how family members want to respond to God's action among them.

Many families may not be accustomed to thinking of God as always (and already) at work in the midst of family life. Pastors who assume that God is always at work in a family can help family members understand that everything working to make their life together more abundant and fulfilling indicates God's presence among them. Likewise, the efforts of family members "to deepen their love for one another, to make their communion stronger and more enriching, is a response to the primary action of God."[3] A family that asks for help with its spiritual life is responding to God's presence and action within the family system, providing a foundation for spiritual development through the process of spiritual direction.

HELPING FAMILIES UNDERSTAND THEIR SPIRITUALITIES

Many families, however, are not aware of how spirituality influences the roles, rituals, and interactions that make up family life. Two tools of long-term marriage and family therapy—genograms and ecomaps—can be adapted by pastors during brief spiritual direction to help families understand their spiritualities. Many pastors are familiar with these tools, though perhaps not in the context of spirituality; usually, genograms and ecomaps are used to help families understand the relationships between different generations of a family and between a family and other social institutions. When used in brief spiritual direction, however, these tools help a family see where its unique spirituality has come from and how that spirituality influences relationships between family members and between the family as a unit and other institutions that influence its life.

Genograms

A *genogram* is a type of family tree that illustrates the relationships among several generations of one family. Usually, a genogram consists of at least three generations: a married couple, the couple's children, and the couple's parents and siblings. When used to explore a family's spirituality, a genogram will include important religious events (for example, interfaith marriages, baptisms, schisms within a church or family, and conversion events), the religious/spiritual orientations of each member, arrows indicating spiritual closeness between family members, dotted lines indicating spiritual distance between family members, and wavy lines indicating spiritual/religious conflict between family members.[4]

Pastors generate a spiritual genogram by drawing the family tree on paper, using circles to represent women and squares to represent men. A horizontal line between a couple indicates marriage, and children (represented by circles or squares, depending on their sex) are placed below the couple and connected by vertical lines to the horizontal marriage line. The couple's own parents are drawn above the couple, joined by horizontal marriage lines and connected to the couple with vertical lines. Siblings of each member of the couple may also be included on the genogram. Then, using information provided by the family, the pastor uses words and symbols to record the information described in the previous paragraph, "mapping" the relationships among family members.

Once the spiritual genogram is drawn and the information recorded, pastors can guide reflection on the diagram to deepen a family's understanding of its spiritual history and its current spirituality. Marsha Wiggins Frame suggests the following questions:

- When you were growing up, what role, if any, did religion/spirituality play in your life? What role does it play now?
- What specific religious/spiritual beliefs do you consider most important for you now? How are those beliefs a source of connection or conflict between you and other family members?

- What religious/spiritual rituals did you participate in as a child or adolescent? How important were they in your family of origin? Which ones do you still engage in? Which ones have let you go? What new rituals have you adopted as an adult? How do these rituals connect you to your religious/spiritual belief system?
- What did/does your religious/spiritual tradition say about gender? About ethnicity? About sexual orientation? How have these beliefs affected you and your extended family?
- What patterns of behavior and relationship resulting from religion/spirituality emerge for you as you study your genogram? How are you currently maintaining or diverting from those patterns?
- How does your religious/spiritual history connect you with your current distress or with the problem you presented for therapy? What new insights or solution may occur to you based on the discoveries you made through the genogram?[5]

Other important questions could focus on strengths or resources available to the family through its spiritual/religious heritages. For example, a pastor might ask a couple how its spiritual heritage provides a foundation for addressing marital conflicts; likewise, pastors might ask a family what gifts God has given it through previous generations. Once spiritual strengths and resources have been identified, pastors can inquire about how those strengths and resources influence the family's spiritual life now, and how family members hope those strengths and resources will influence their spiritual lives in the future.

Ecomaps

Ecomaps can be another tool for understanding a family's spirituality. Ecomaps diagram the relationships among a family system (usually just two generations: parents and their children); social institutions, such as the church; and other environmental systems, such as schools, employers, and groups of friends. The household is represented by a large circle placed at the center of the ecomap; smaller circles around the household system represent the systems and institutions to which the household relates. A spiritual ecomap can include circles representing rituals, the spiritual traditions of the couple's parents' congregations, God, and other important systems, figures, and people influencing the family's spirituality.

Once the appropriate systems and institutions are drawn on the ecomap, lines and symbols are drawn to show relationships—good, bad, strong, weak, and so forth—among the systems and institutions, the household as a whole, and individual family members. Important dates and events (such as conversions and baptisms) are recorded as well. Stories about the relationship illustrated on the ecomap can be tapped by the pastor to help a family understand its spiritual history, its current spirituality, and the resources available to it through its religious/spiritual heritages.

FAMILY SPIRITUALITY IN THE CHRISTIAN TRADITIONS

In spiritual direction with couples and families, pastors can help families understand and deepen their spirituality by teaching them about the church's historic approaches to the subject. The family has been considered both a unique setting for God's revelation and a community in which God's work can be known. A family's spirituality is demonstrated in the way its members relate to one another and to their neighbors. A spiritually centered family "responds to the creative healing and renewing energies of the Spirit [and as] a result it is able to turn outward to church and community in responsible, caring ways."[6] Attending to the ways family members respond in the family and in the community to God's presence and action can be an important way of assessing the health and effectiveness of a family's spiritual life.

Christianity has always considered families important (if not essential) to the work of the church and to the spiritual growth of an individual. Historically, early monastic patterns of worship, prayer, and work were used as a template to shape family life. Morning and evening prayer, grace before meals, religious instruction, and singing hymns were common family activities. The home was considered a training ground for learning obedience to God.[7] In the Catholic tradition, the family has been considered both a guardian of solitude, where family members are given time and space to listen for and follow the call of God (thus becoming the people God intends them to be), and a center of intimacy and hospitality, where family members perfect the art of Christian love.[8] In the twenty-first century, family spirituality may require us, as Ernest Boyer Jr. suggests, to dedicate ourselves "to live the daily expressions of two sacraments, the sacrament of the care of others and the sacrament of routine. They are both hard sacraments to live, but within the first love is revealed and within the second the sacredness of ordinary activity. To live both together is to find in the truest manner possible the presence of

God."[9] It is in a family's daily life, then, that spiritual values such as faithfulness, mutuality, prayerful discernment, and seeking the kingdom of God are taught and modeled so that its members participate in the work of Christ.

LIVING IN THE PRESENCE OF GOD

Family members may not intentionally attend to their relationships with God, either as individuals or as a family. They may have forgotten that they live always in the presence of God, because (with the possible exception of Sunday morning) they do not pause to reflect on God's presence or to communicate with God daily. Thus, the family's structure and its interactions fail to make room for the relationship that grounds all relationships. The family does not know (or has forgotten) that spirituality is a way of life, rather than a set of religious behaviors limited to particular times or places.

For such families, a pastor's first step in providing brief spiritual direction may be to identify ways of *opening contemplative space*—creating times and places where the family can attend to its relationship with God in order to remind family members that they live in the presence of a God who is actively involved in the family. The prayer of quiet, the practice of the presence of God, observation of the Sabbath, family worship, hospitality, and family retreats are all practices from the Christian tradition for opening contemplative space. A pastor can easily teach these practices to couples and families.

The Prayer of Quiet

One of the easiest interventions pastors can suggest is the prayer of quiet: setting aside the chaos of family life for a brief time each day (five minutes is sufficient, especially in the beginning) to sit together in silence. Family members can breathe deeply together, silently repeating a word or phrase to themselves (such as "peace" or "love" or "be still and know"). They can end the time by reciting the Lord's Prayer.

The prayer of quiet works best when it becomes a natural part of the family's routine. For this reason, it must be integrated into the rhythms of the family's life. Trying to squeeze five minutes of silence into a hectic morning routine of preparing for work and school, for example, may bring more stress than benefit to a family. Placing the prayer of quiet at the end of the day, when everyone is slowing down and getting ready to sleep, might make better sense. Some families may want to add the prayer of quiet to the blessing of the evening meal or to the baby's bath time. The important thing is that the prayer of quiet should fit naturally into the family's routine so that it can become an anticipated time of corporate worship rather than another distraction in a busy life.

Creating sacred space in which to practice the prayer of quiet can also be helpful. Families might create a sacred space in the home by using a kneeling bench, laying down a special rug during prayer, lighting candles and focusing on religious symbols to establish a prayerful mood, or burning incense to mark the transition from "ordinary time" to "sacred time." Having a sacred space in the home, and using it daily, helps establish the space as a spot where people can go to be free from the intrusions of others. Having such a space in the family home communicates the importance of spending time in the presence of God and respecting the silent prayer of others. Entering the sacred space also provides a way for family members to signal when they are in need of prayer or other spiritual support from those they love and live among.

Practicing the Presence of God

The Christian traditions have always emphasized that living with awareness of the presence of God takes *practice.* Likewise, family members are called to practice the sacrament of caring for others and the sacrament of routine, attending to God's presence as they help with the children's homework and dress the toddler, load the dishwasher and sweep the kitchen, say good-bye in the morning and distribute mail in the afternoon. To help sanctify such daily rhythms and family interactions, pastors can teach parents, spouses, and other family members a modified version of the "practice of the presence of God," which was developed by Brother Lawrence, a seventeenth-century Carmelite monk who served as a spiritual director to many.

This practice, as modified by Boyer, entails four steps: (1) pausing to reflect on God's presence before beginning an activity or exchange with a family member, (2) repeating a short prayer (such as "Lord Jesus Christ, have mercy on me" or "Peace be with you") during the activity, (3) reflecting at the end of the task or exchange, and (4) working to carry prayer and reflection into all activities related to the family and household maintenance. For example, a father who is bathing an infant might pause to think about God's presence before turning on the water; during the bath, he might reflect on the symbolism of water as purification, prayerfully cleaning his son or daughter; and after the bath, he might give thanks for the opportunity to be present with his child and with

God during a mundane activity. Then he could carry the contemplative awareness of God's presence into his other activities for the evening, such as reading a bedtime story, rocking the baby to sleep, and preparing bottles for the coming day.

Keeping the Sabbath

The Sabbath is a day of rest and re-creation, a time set aside to remember God and God's actions on behalf of the world. Judaism celebrates the Sabbath from sundown Friday to sundown Saturday; Christianity celebrates it on Sunday. While it may be difficult to set aside a whole day, a family can remember and keep the Sabbath in a modified fashion, perhaps by lighting a candle and saying a short prayer at dinner Friday or Saturday evening or by always having a spiritually informed family activity or a mission project (such as working at a food bank) planned for Saturday morning or Sunday afternoon.

The importance of Sabbath keeping is that the family is reminded weekly of the primacy of its relationship to God, the call to be faithful to one another, and the responsibility to reach out to others. Observing the Sabbath can also be an important way of teaching children about their religious heritages and about the family's commitment to God, to worship, and to being together prayerfully. While keeping the Sabbath is a serious commitment, it should be celebratory, not dreary. It can include intentional play, spiritually attuned movies, walks in nature, simple and nutritious meals, or just time and space to rest together.

Family Worship

Another way to open contemplative space is to encourage the family to worship together at home. Different family members can plan each service. Family worship can be as simple as a shared devotion at the breakfast table or prayers before bed. The creation of rituals and traditions can be particularly important for the family's life-cycle events (birthdays, anniversaries, graduations) and for ordinary, repetitive times together (such as rituals around making a meal together or having a family meeting in which each person shares the week's highlights and concerns).

Such services should be short and simple and involve as many family members as possible in reading Scripture, saying a blessing, or performing a small task. It is fine to repeat prayers or use the same liturgy over and over; such repetition can be comforting and can help establish worship as a tradition. Children should be involved in some significant way rather than being expected to simply observe the worship led by parents. Friends, relatives, and neighbors may be invited to join in family worship, followed by a communally prepared meal.

Hospitality

Reaching out to others is a central virtue of Christian life, and nurturing hospitality within the family deepens the family's spiritual life and focuses the family on something other than its own problems. Hospitality can include volunteering, being polite to others, and inviting guests to the home. The emphasis should be less on "doing things for others" than on "making a gift of our time" out of a commitment to love as Christ loves.

Family Retreats

A pastor might also suggest a family retreat—not a vacation, but time designated for parents and children to be together in God's presence for an extended time. This can take place at a camp, a retreat center, or even in the family home. A retreat should be carefully planned so it does not become entertainment; a family retreat emphasizes *being* as well as *doing*—for example, walking quietly together, playing volleyball after a time of prayer, or sharing a meal by candlelight after singing together.

The agenda for a family retreat should include lots of free, unstructured time together and apart. Simple worship services, as described earlier, are appropriate as is sharing Bible stories and conversation about one another's lives with God. The important part of a retreat is being together in the presence of God, aware of how God participates in the life of the family.

GOD'S ROLE IN THE FAMILY: FAMILY SYSTEMS THOUGHT

Ideas from the practice of marriage and family counseling, especially family systems thought, can enhance the practice of spiritual guidance with families. Systems thought challenges us to see God as *a part of the family system*. For many families, God functions as "a crucial family member" involved in daily family interactions.[10] God's day-to-day involvement in the family system means spirituality is built into the activities and interactions of the family members.

When a family is facing difficulties, a pastor can strengthen family members' relationships with one another by focusing on God's role in that family *as manifested in the relationship between each family member and God.* Attention to the relationship between God and individual family members can produce change in family behaviors. Pastors may especially focus on two areas. First, pastors may attend to the family's religious belief system, religious roles, religious rules, and religious patterns—for example, does the family's faith teach that the husband should always make the decisions about money? Does the faith community to which the family belongs emphasize obedience over grace? Are confession and forgiveness an important part of the family's religious heritage? Second, pastors may attend to the way each individual in the family conceives of and interacts with God—for example, how does each family member imagine God might look? How do family members think God feels about them? What is the pattern of prayer and worship in each family member's private life?

Three marriage and family counseling approaches that pastors may use in brief spiritual direction with a family are questioning, differentiation, and heightened awareness of differences.

Questioning

Questions from the pastor can be used to influence a family and its spirituality by changing the way family members view people and situations. Such questions particularly help with discerning a family's response to God's action and presence in their lives. Questions may include (or be similar to) the following:

- How do you think God feels about you when you interact with your spouse this way?
- In the future, if you behave in ways consistent with who you believe God wants you to be, how might you act differently in a similar situation?
- Can you describe what happened between you as God might have seen it? If both of you had understood the interaction that way, what might have been different? How might you have acted differently?
- Has there ever been a time when God gave you the power to act differently—for example, to clean up the kitchen or not to fight with or cheat on your spouse? What was different about that time? How might you tap into that power in the future?

To be successful, such questions should address (1) the spiritual/religious meaning each person makes of family interactions or events, (2) the role of God as an autonomous member of the family system, and (3) specific new behaviors that result from a new understanding of God's involvement, perspective, or desire in relation to the family's presenting difficulties.

Differentiation

For couples who have a shared belief (as evidenced by mutual prayer, shared participation in religious ritual, and a common language and understanding about their spiritual lives), God may have more influence in the marriage than any other family member. According to Mark Butler and James Harper, "Symbols, rituals and daily routine suggest that, in the religious marriage, God operates *more nearly and regularly within* the marital boundaries than perhaps any other person, including the extended-family members."[11]

For such couples, God maintains a closeness to the marital pair and promotes individual responsibility within the marriage.[12] Thus, in spiritual direction, the pastor can draw on Scripture, tradition, and the couple's understanding of God to promote processes related to *differentiation*, a term from family systems thought that addresses the capacity of each partner to define life goals and values apart from the other partner or the rest of the family.[13] A key to differentiation is to remain connected to others in a relaxed way even if conflict or anxiety exists in the marriage or the family.

When providing spiritual guidance to a couple or to families with relationships that are highly conflicted or anxious and in which each person reacts to another's emotions in unhealthy ways, the pastor can suggest that each family member focus less on others and more on his or her relationship with God. This may increase differentiation and diffuse anxiety between the couple.

Heightening Awareness of Differences

For families that prefer to keep spirituality private rather than shared, or for marriages in which one partner is more spiritually active or mature than the other, the pastor can still focus attention on God's role in the family system. This can be accomplished through (1) questions that make explicit the different ways in which family members think about and experience God and their spiritual lives, and (2) questions that clarify what family members think God expects of them as individuals and as a family.

Pastors should avoid both making efforts to convert a "less spiritual" spouse and speaking words that condemn a "sinning" family member.

Rather, pastors must focus on questions that make each family member's experiences and understandings of God as explicit as possible. Helping family members claim their own experiences and understandings of God can help the differentiation of individuals in the family.

CONSIDERING THE FAMILY'S VOCATION IN SPIRITUAL DIRECTION

God calls a couple or family to a particular vocation or purpose. Considering this vocation can be an important aspect of providing spiritual direction to a family or couple. John Welwood argues that "what can sustain a couple when all else fails is knowing that they are together *for a larger purpose.*"[14]

To focus on a family's vocation, the pastor can ask a couple to reflect, individually and together, on why God has called them into relationship—what it is they are to accomplish as a couple or family. Together, they can write a shared statement of purpose for their marriage, a provisional understanding of what God is calling them to at that particular time and place. Later, if the couple encounters struggles in their marriage, the couple—with the guidance of the pastor—can return to the statement of purpose and ask, "How might we get through this situation in a way that is true to God's purpose for our marriage?" A family retreat might be a good time to reflect on the vocation of a family or marriage and to write a statement of purpose.

CONCLUSION: AFFIRMING "SYSTEMIC SPIRITUALITY"

The Christian spiritual traditions contain significant resources for pastors providing spiritual guidance to couples and families. These resources, unlike most marriage and family therapy literature, recognize and build on a family's relationship to God. Continued integration of the relational aspects of Christian spirituality into the way pastors care for marriages and families can provide important resources for pastors who take seriously their responsibility to care for family systems and not just individuals.

9

DISCOVERING YOUR PURPOSE: EXPLORING VOCATION IN SHORT-TERM GROUP SPIRITUAL DIRECTION

Feeling unwanted and distant from God, Tom was searching for a way to connect with the Spirit and understand his purpose in life. Sandy hoped to identify God's actions in her past and thus discover new directions for the future. Joan was struggling to discern whether a new career opportunity was consistent with her Christian vocation.

All three of them realized their goals in a six-week spiritual direction group called Discovering Your Purpose, which focused on the doctrine of vocation. Through directed meditation and the support of his peers, Tom heard God call him "a gift to the world"—an experience that created a new self-image and affirmed his value despite ongoing struggles with childhood abuse. Sandy developed a new sense of God's ongoing presence and activity in her life, knowing (and trusting!) for the first time that God was leading her journey. Joan turned down a coveted job because her group experience significantly altered the way she thinks of her career and her purpose as a Christian.

This chapter offers a blueprint for Discovering Your Purpose, the group in which they participated. I developed and facilitated the group in partnership with Lee Self, a Disciples of Christ (Christian Church) minister and retreat leader, at the Pastoral Care and Training Center in Fort Worth, Texas.

GOD'S CALL IN COMMUNITY

The group was built on the Reformed doctrine of *vocation*, which posits that God has given a unique call to each individual. That call includes a specific ministry within the church as well as the responsibility of being a witness to God's truth in everyday life—for example, while shopping at the grocery store, working in the office, cooking dinner, or driving along the freeway. An individual's call appears first as an inner prompting and then as an outer call affirmed by the faith community. The doctrine of vocation is related to Martin Luther's idea of the priesthood of all believers, in which each Christian is called to contribute to God's work in the world.

While it is important for people to be intentional about discerning God's call in their lives through prayer and meditation (the inner call), it is also important that they offer that call for group discernment (the outer call). Thus, the Discovering Your Purpose group asks people to spend time with God both alone and as a community and then to reflect together on those experiences. This rhythm of solitary prayer followed by group participation offers structure and accountability for the discernment process. In the process, people can be empowered both to know, live, and share the life of God in new ways and to risk more in relationships.

CHOOSING PARTICIPANTS

For the group to succeed, expectations for participants must be clear and the group must be right for each person's needs. Thus, the spiritual director should meet with each individual prior to the first group session. This meeting serves several purposes, including

- to help the director understand each person's experiences with spiritual formation and to stimulate that person's thinking about those experiences
- to allow the director to answer questions about the group and be explicit about the required homework and the level of commitment expected of group members (discussed below)
- to help directors clarify that Discovering Your Purpose is not a counseling group and does not focus on crises or prolonged difficulties in individual's lives
- to provide an opportunity to review confidentiality requirements and to discuss the fee, if any, for the group

Participants are expected to attend at least five of six group sessions, to complete spiritual exercises at home each week, to share their experience with the group, to write their spiritual journey (one to five pages) to share with the group, to create a purpose statement to share with the group, and to complete an evaluation.

GROUP CONTEXT AND STRUCTURE

The group, which is made up of no more than twelve people, meets weekly for two hours. While no specific religious commitment is required, the group is based on Christian spiritual traditions and is organized around six themes: understanding the concept of call or vocation, searching, listening, clarifying, acting, and writing a statement of purpose. One theme is presented each week. The themes reflect the discernment process that group members learn through participation.

A consistent weekly format helps create feelings of safety, security, and trust. While the format is flexible, it also requires the facilitator to trust God's ability to fill and direct the group. The weekly schedule includes the following:

- Gathering to music, followed by silence and centering
- Opening song
- Administrative concerns (fees, schedule changes, and so forth)
- Sharing of "joys and concerns," followed by prayer
- Reflections and responses to the previous week's lesson and exercises
- Exploration of a new topic (including an experiential prayer exercise, introduction of material for the coming week, distribution of handouts, and questions/answers)
- Closing song
- Recitation of the Lord's Prayer

The group succeeds to the degree that it opens space for reflection on and response to the experiences of group members as they explore various spiritual disciplines and exercises. Participants must feel free to share observations, dreams, songs, and significant memories.

The name of the group is also important to its success. Not only does the phrase "Discovering Your Purpose" clarify that the emphasis is self-exploration toward a clearer understanding of God's will for each person's life, but it also helps make the group cohesive by attracting people with a shared interest.

WEEKLY EXERCISES

Weekly exercises are the key to sparking individual and group experiences that evoke understanding and insight, enhance learning, and sharpen each participant's understanding of his or her call. Each week's topic and exercises are discussed below.

Week One: Call/Vocation

The first meeting features a brief discussion of the concept of call or vocation, followed by each participant's sharing of a reason for attending the group. Then the group facilitators share the story of their spiritual journeys, striving to model openness and intimacy for the group.

During the session, participants talk about the idea of the universe as a place of learning—that an intelligent God has designed it for a purpose, that it is moving toward a desired goal, and that this intelligent God is aware of each individual, has given each person a unique purpose, and helps each person learn what that purpose is. The biblical stories of Paul, Mary and Martha, and Sarah and Abraham are referenced as examples of people being called to attend to the purpose that God has designed for them (and designed them for!). Psalm 139, which speaks of the presence of God in creation, may be used as a group reading.

As a take-home exercise, participants prepare to share their personal stories with the group. Questions to guide their reflection can be provided on a handout. Helpful questions include the following:

- What does it feel like to be filled with a purpose?
- When have you had a sense of "calling" to some purpose?
- In what way is your own life a "teaching" from God?
- What have you learned so far?
- What have been the "stops along the way" in your spiritual journey? Where have you come from, where have you visited, and where are you headed?

Week Two: Searching

At the second meeting, group members share their own stories and listen to reflections from the larger group. Each person shares his or her story within a set period of time (ten to fifteen minutes), then the group members share their responses to the story. As the group reflects, it is important that participants remain "tentative" in their comments—for example, wondering about aspects of a person's story, asking gentle questions, sharing impressions and emotional responses—rather than making definitive statements about what a person's experiences mean or offering advice about what the person should do. Sharing and listening carefully are time-consuming activities, so it is best to forgo an experiential exercise at the second meeting.

The take-home exercise for this meeting focuses on the metaphor of searching. The spiritual search is spoken of as a journey, for which people must be prepared, just as they would plan and prepare for a camping trip. The provisions taken on this journey must be balanced and carefully chosen. They must address the needs and demands of the journey, and they must be tailored to each individual's particular trip. On their own time, participants reflect on, pray about, and journal on the following themes:

- Spiritual "parents"—those people who helped "birth" and "grow" them as spiritual beings
- Sources of spiritual nutrition in their lives, such as Scripture, worship, meditation, and prayer
- Patterns of communication and dialogue with God and others, such as prayer, silence, conversation, and physical activities
- Rhythms of rest, silence, and order in their lives
- The value of spiritual work done alone and on behalf of others.[1]

Week Three: Listening

After sharing what they learned in the previous week about the provisions they have used on their spiritual journeys and what provisions they need to stock up on for the future, participants engage in an experiential exercise on listening. Closing their eyes and relaxing their bodies, they focus on their breath and begin to pay attention to the different things they can hear with their bodies, minds, and souls. Conversation after the exercise may focus on what the experience was like for participants. It is also important to reflect together on how easy it is to be distracted by everything clamoring for our attention—something group members will have clearly experienced during their focused meditation.

After the discussion, the facilitator talks briefly about listening for the voice of God in different ways—for example, in Scripture, in creation, through one another, through the circumstances of our lives, and through journaling. Take-home exercises ask participants to commit to spending at least fifteen minutes each day listening to God and then fifteen minutes journaling about their experiences of listening. Suggested ways of listening to God include praying at every moment, "Lord, what should I do?"; sitting in silence while focusing on the breath and repeating a word or brief prayer of their choosing; and looking for God's will for their lives as expressed in Scripture, creation, the people they encounter, and the circumstances of their lives. During the exercise, participants focus on listening for a sense of call or vocation.[2]

Week Four: Clarifying

As usual, participants begin the meeting by sharing what they heard from God during the previous week. Then the group participates in a visualization prayer based on the Ignatian exercises. In the prayer, led by the facilitator, participants imagine a statue of their life and then imagine Jesus changing the statue in some way (see chapter 6). This exercise can be the most powerful experience of the six-week group. For many group members, it may become a touchstone for understanding their call or vocation.

After sharing their experiences of the visualization and reflecting on one another's stories, the group learns about the importance of clarifying what they hear from God in consultation with others. The conversation emphasizes the importance of a trusted community of believers to "test" a person's understanding of what is heard during periods of prayer. This testing can occur through conversation with others, reading the testimonies of others, and reflecting on Scripture. Clarity cannot be found alone; in community, we find strength, faith, healing, and growth.

The take-home exercise is to take what has been learned in listening to God during the previous week and during this week's guided meditation and to offer it to another person the participant trusts. The participant asks that person for thoughts, encouragement, or concerns raised by what is shared. This is often the first time participants share their prayer lives with another person, and it can be important to take some time talking about the anxiety and fear that this exercise may trigger.

Week Five: Acting

After debriefing the previous week's take-home exercise, the facilitators share their statements of purpose and ask for feedback from the group. Again, the facilitators seek to model how group members might approach sharing their own statements of purpose. Some group members might not feel as if they have heard enough from God to write a statement of purpose; therefore, it may help to emphasize that God expects us to act even though we have only a partial understanding of our purpose or role in life.

Group members are then challenged to act on their reflections from the previous weeks by writing a statement of purpose as their take-home exercise. This challenge includes a recognition that understanding one's mission or vocation is a lifelong task that shifts as we see more (or less) clearly at different places in our journey. Thus, writing a statement of purpose is an ongoing process; the product is always partial and open to revision. The final product might be a poem, a "recipe" for life, a T-shirt slogan, a sculpture or collage, a painting, or a set of goals.

Before writing a statement of purpose, each person should spend some time in prayer and discernment, reviewing the work done in the group during the previous four weeks—the prayer forms used, the new ways in which God has spoken, the sorts of messages received, the observations of others who know the individual. Suggestions for a statement of purpose include the following:

- Focusing both on who you are called to be (your character) and what you are called to do (your contributions and achievements)
- Using active verbs—"doing," "working," and "praying"—rather than passive verbs
- Distilling the statement to its essence (something that would fit on a T-shirt)
- Communicating a sense of what your life *means*—to you, to others, and to God
- Attending to both inner and outer dimensions of purpose—not only who you are as a child of God but what you are called to do in the world and how you will affect others
- Having fun, being creative, and remaining playful about creating a statement on which to center your life at this point in time.

It is important to ask participants to be intentional about reflecting on what they need from the group when they share their statement of purpose in the final session. Are they looking for general feedback, affirmation, suggestions for action, or prayers? Would they like group members to challenge them or, instead, to support them where they are?

Week Six: Statements of Purpose

In the final session, each group member shares the statement of purpose that evolved out of participation in the group. These statements may be either written or represented in some other art form.

THE TAPESTRY: STATEMENTS OF PURPOSE

For the participants in our spiritual direction group, emotions ran high during the final session, in which they shared their statements of purpose. Tom brought a song that reflected how he felt God was feeling about him; Sandy created a three-dimensional collage of fabric, fur, and metal to represent the different eras of her life and her future directions. Joan wrote a chant that reminded her of her Christian call. Confidentiality prevents me from being specific, but each group member felt a significant shift in understanding his or her place in the world. In many ways, the statements of purpose challenged group members to make their gifts available to the community as a whole.

As emphasized earlier, a statement of purpose is never finished but acts as a touchstone for a certain time in a person's life. A statement of purpose can be used to make decisions about jobs and careers, places to live and study, or people who might become friends and companions. Such a statement is never written in stone; it may change tremendously over a lifetime as we gather experiences and wisdom, yet it can give direction to a life and ground it in what we have understood God to say about our particular activities and commitments. Knowledge of our purpose is never complete, but we must act on the information and understanding available *at this point in time.*

KEEPING TRACK

Directors should ask group participants to arrange an individual meeting halfway through the group's time together. This allows the director to check in and assess, outside of the group setting, how the material is affecting each participant. As pastors, it is important for directors to keep track of how spiritual direction—whether offered individually or in a group setting—is shaping the members of the church and others who may come for guidance on their spiritual journeys.

NOTES

PREFACE

1. See Kenneth Leech, *Soul Friend: An Invitation to Spiritual Direction* (San Francisco: HarperSanFrancisco, 1980), 85ff.

1. THE MINISTRY OF SPIRITUAL DIRECTION

1. For a more thorough look at the complex history and nature of spiritual direction, readers might explore Kenneth Leech's classic, *Soul Friend: An Invitation to Spiritual Direction* (San Francisco: HarperSanFrancisco, 1980), and Tilden Edwards's *Spiritual Friend: Reclaiming the Gift of Spiritual Direction* (New York: Paulist, 1980).

2. William A. Barry and William J. Connolly, *The Practice of Spiritual Direction* (San Francisco: HarperSanFrancisco, 1986), 8; emphasis in original.

3. Jeannette A. Bakke, *Holy Invitations: Exploring Spiritual Direction* (Grand Rapids: Baker, 2000), 28–29; emphasis in original.

4. Phil Marshall Negley, "The First Steps of the Journey: The Historical-Theological Metaphor of Pilgrimage and the Charism and Ministry of Initial Spiritual Direction" (Ph.D. diss., Andover Newton Theological School, 1996), 107.

5. Thomas Dubay, *Seeking Spiritual Direction: How to Grow the Divine Life Within* (Ann Arbor: Servant, 1993), 55–62.

6. Josef Sudbrack, *Spiritual Guidance*, trans. Peter Heinegg (New York: Paulist, 1983), 22.

7. Thomas Merton, *Spiritual Direction and Meditation* (Collegeville, Minn.: Liturgical, 1960), 17.

8. Joseph J. Allen, *Inner Way: Toward a Rebirth of Eastern Spiritual Direction* (Grand Rapids: Eerdmans, 1994), 133.

9. Muriel Heppell, "The Role of the Spiritual Father in Orthodox Monasticism," in *Monastic Studies: The Continuity of Tradition*, vol. 2, ed. Judith Loades (Bangor, Gwynedd, Wales: Headstart History, 1991), 23–24.

10. See Howard W. Stone, *Brief Pastoral Counseling: Short-Term Approaches and Strategies* (Minneapolis: Fortress Press, 1994), vii. See also Howard W. Stone, ed., *Strategies for Brief Pastoral Counseling* (Minneapolis: Fortress Press, 2001).

116 NOTES

11. Adrian van Kaam, *Dynamics of Spiritual Self-Direction* (Denville, N.J.: Dimension, 1976), 12.

12. Kevin G. Culligan, "The Counseling Ministry and Spiritual Direction," in *Pastoral Counseling*, ed. Barry K. Estadt, Melvin Blanchette, and John R. Compton (Englewood Cliffs, N.J.: Prentice-Hall, 1983), 41.

13. Hubert S. Box, *Spiritual Direction: A Short Introduction to the* Ars Artium Regimen Animarum (London: SPCK, 1938), 50; Kenneth Leech, *Spirituality and Pastoral Care* (Cambridge: Cowley, 1989), 48–49.

14. Peter Verity, "Spiritual Direction in the Single Meeting," *The Way Supplement* 54 (1985): 21–29.

15. Ibid.

2. KNOWING UNKNOWING

1. James W. Fowler, *Stages of Faith: The Psychology of Human Development and the Quest for Meaning* (San Francisco: Harper & Row, 1981). See also James W. Fowler, *Faith Development and Pastoral Care*, Theology and Pastoral Care (Philadelphia: Fortress Press, 1987).

2. Harlene Anderson and Harold Goolishian, "The Client Is the Expert: A Not-Knowing Approach to Therapy," in *Therapy as Social Construction*, ed. Sheila McNamee and Kenneth J. Gergen (London: Sage, 1992), 37.

3. Lynn Hoffman, "A Reflexive Stance for Family Therapy," in *Therapy as Social Construction*, ed. McNamee and Gergen, 7–24; Anderson and Goolishian, "The Client Is the Expert," 25–39.

4. Harlene Anderson, *Conversation, Language, and Possibilities: A Postmodern Approach to Therapy* (New York: Basic, 1997), 140.

5. Richard Woods, *Mysticism and Prophecy: The Dominican Tradition*, Traditions of Christian Spirituality, ed. Philip Sheldrake (Maryknoll, N.Y.: Orbis, 1998), 14.

6. Nicholas of Cusa in Jasper Hopkins, *Nicholas of Cusa on Learned Ignorance: A Translation and an Appraisal of De Docta Ignorantia* (Minneapolis: Banning, 1985), 50–51.

7. Woods, *Mysticism and Prophecy*, 134.

8. Ibid., 135.

9. Donald Capps, *Pastoral Counseling and Preaching: A Quest for an Integrated Ministry* (Philadelphia: Westminster, 1980), 10.

10. Sarah Coakley, "*Kenosis* and Subversion," in *Swallowing a Fishbone? Feminist Theologians Debate Christianity*, ed. Daphne Hampson (London: SPCK, 1996), 89; emphasis in original.

11. Ibid.; emphasis in original.

12. Ibid., 84; emphasis in original.

13. Ibid., 88; emphasis in original.

14. Ibid., 107.

15. Ibid.

16. Ibid.

17. Ibid.; emphasis in original.

18. Anderson, *Conversation, Language, and Possibilities*, 247–48.

19. Ibid., 134–36.

20. I am indebted to Lynn Bauman, ascetical theologian and priest in the Oriental Orthodox tradition, for this line of thinking.

21. I am grateful to colleagues Nancy J. Gorsuch and Frank N. Thomas for introducing me to this concept. See Nancy J. Gorsuch, "Collaborative Pastoral Conversation," in *Strategies for Brief Pastoral Counseling*, ed. Howard W. Stone (Minneapolis: Fortress Press, 2001), 31.

3. GUIDANCE FROM BRIEF PASTORAL COUNSELING

1. These psychotherapeutic models focus on people's existing strengths and resources rather than on deficits by identifying the "hidden expertise" and "subjugated stories" in people's lives. In contrast to psychodynamic models, these models of care assume people are competent to address their own difficulties and focus on the present and future rather than the past. The therapist's expertise, as discussed in chapter 2, lies not in seeing things more clearly than the counselee but in managing a process through which people discover their own resources.

2. See Charles Allen Kollar, *Solution-Focused Pastoral Counseling: An Effective Short-Term Approach for Getting People Back on Track* (Grand Rapids: Zondervan, 1997); Gary J. Oliver, Monte Hasz, and Matthew Richburg, *Promoting Change through Brief Therapy in Christian Counseling* (Wheaton, Ill.: Tyndale, 1997); and Frank N. Thomas and Jack Cockburn, *Competency-Based Counseling: Building on Client Strengths*, Creative Pastoral Care and Counseling (Minneapolis: Fortress Press, 1998).

3. For a more thorough critique of these assumptions in light of Christian theology, see Duane R. Bidwell, "Hope and Possibility: The Theology of Culture Inherent to Solution-Focused Brief Therapy," *American Journal of Pastoral Counseling* 3/1 (2000): 3–21.

4. In Jerome N. Neufelder and Marcy C. Coelho, eds., *Writings on Spiritual Direction by Great Christian Masters* (New York: Seabury, 1982), 97.

4. THE FIRST SESSION

1. Thomas Dubay, *Seeking Spiritual Direction: How to Grow the Divine Life Within* (Ann Arbor: Servant, 1993), 55–62.

2. Peter Verity, "Spiritual Direction in the Single Meeting," *The Way Supplement* 54 (1985): 21–29.

3. William A. Barry and William J. Connolly, *The Practice of Spiritual Direction* (San Francisco: HarperSanFrancisco, 1995), 70.

5. TAKING ACTION:
TECHNIQUES FROM BRIEF PASTORAL COUNSELING

1. Alan Jones in Margaret Guenther, *Holy Listening: The Art of Spiritual Direction* (Cambridge, Mass.: Cowley, 1992), ix.

2. Alan Jones, *Exploring Spiritual Direction: An Essay on Christian Friendship* (New York: Seabury, 1982), 1–2.

3. Joseph J. Allen, *Inner Way: Toward a Rebirth of Eastern Christian Spiritual Direction* (Grand Rapids: Eerdmans, 1994), 133.

4. Robert F. Morneau, *Spiritual Direction: Principles and Practices* (New York: Crossroad, 1992), 29.

5. See Allen, *Inner Way,* 87; and Ester de Waal, *The Way of Simplicity: The Cistercian Tradition,* Traditions of Christian Spirituality (Maryknoll, N.Y.: Orbis, 1998), 15.

6. Gordon Jeff, *Spiritual Direction for Every Christian* (London: SPCK, 1987), 25–26.

6. CONTEMPLATIVE ACTION: INTERVENTIONS
FROM THE SPIRITUAL TRADITIONS

1. See Robert Morneau, *Spiritual Direction: Principles and Practices* (New York: Crossroad, 1992), 101–2.

2. People can silently say, "Lord Jesus Christ, Son of God," as they breathe in; as they breathe out, they can silently pray, "have mercy on me." Some traditions add the phrase "a sinner" at the end of the prayer: "Lord Jesus Christ, Son of God, have mercy on me, a sinner."

3. Roberta Bondi, *To Love as God Loves: Conversations with the Early Church* (Philadelphia: Fortress Press, 1987), 78, emphasis in original.

4. A strong sense of shame in relation to a particular passion is a sign that the passion has some power or influence over a person. The intensity of shame can reflect the intensity with which the passion has a hold over the person's thoughts, words, and actions—that is, the greater the feeling of shame when the passion is named, the more influence that passion may have over the person.

5. See Columba Stewart, *Prayer and Community: The Benedictine Tradition,* Traditions of Christian Spirituality (Maryknoll, N.Y.: Orbis, 1998), 101–2.

6. Margaret Guenther, *Holy Listening: The Art of Spiritual Direction* (Cambridge, Mass.: Cowley, 1992), 28.

7. Richard J. Foster, *Celebration of Discipline: The Path to Spiritual Growth* (rev. and exp. ed.; San Francisco: HarperSanFrancisco, 1988), 149–50.

8. Foster, *Celebration of Discipline*, 156.

9. Joseph D. Driskill, *Protestant Spiritual Exercises: Theology, History, and Practice* (Harrisburg, Pa.: Morehouse, 1999), 89.

10. Margaret Guenther, *Toward Holy Ground: Spiritual Directions for the Second Half of Life* (Cambridge, Mass.: Cowley, 1995), 64.

11. Guenther, *Toward Holy Ground*, 64.

12. Lynn C. Bauman, *The Praxis of Prayer: Exercises in the Art of Christian Praying for Congregational Life* (Telephone, Tex.: Praxis, 1992), 130.

7. THE ART OF DISCERNMENT IN BRIEF SPIRITUAL DIRECTION

1. Maureen Conroy, *The Discerning Heart: Discovering a Personal God* (Chicago: Loyola, 1993), 13.

2. It may be more accurate to speak of "aligning our choices with God's intentions for creation" than "discovering God's will for *me*." Nonetheless, many people do frame the question as one of clarifying what God's will is for them personally. While there are limits to such claims, exploring them is beyond the scope of this text.

3. David C. Duncombe, "Christian Life," in *Dictionary of Pastoral Care and Counseling*, ed. Rodney J. Hunter (Nashville: Abingdon, 1996).

4. See Martin Thornton, "Discernment of Spirits," in *Dictionary of Pastoral Care and Counseling*.

5. Conroy, *The Discerning Heart*, 13–14.

6. See Thornton, "Discernment of Spirits." My list of norms and criteria is paraphrased from his article.

7. Or the desires of negative spiritual energies that may or may not be a part of the person. These energies—or "powers and principalities," to use a Pauline phrase—are phenomena beyond the scope of this text. The patristic literature of the church discusses these energies, which Ignatius calls "the enemy." Depth psychology, while removing them from the realm of "the spiritual," has clarified the role of such energies in human development and experience.

8. Conroy, *The Discerning Heart*, 21.

9. See Gerald May, *Care of Mind, Care of Spirit: Psychiatric Dimensions of Spiritual Direction* (San Francisco: Harper & Row, 1982), 90.

8. SPIRITUAL GUIDANCE WITH COUPLES AND FAMILIES

1. Paul R. Giblin, "Marital Spirituality: A Quantitative Study," *Journal of Religion and Health* 36/4 (1997): 329, emphasis added.

2. Douglas A. Anderson, "Spirituality and Systems Theory: Partners in Clinical Practice," *Journal of Pastoral Psychology* 1/1 (1987): 92.

3. Kenan B. Osborne, "The Theology and Spirituality of Marriage," *Catholic World* 238/1425 (1995): 125.

4. For greater detail about spiritual genograms, readers may consult Marsha Wiggins Frame, "The Spiritual Genogram in Family Therapy," *Journal of Marital and Family Therapy* 26/2 (2000): 211–16. Also see Robert F. Massey and Adriana Balguer Dunn, "Viewing the Transactional Dimensions of Spirituality through Family Prisms," *Transactional Analysis Journal* 29/2 (1999): 115–29.

5. See Frame, "The Spiritual Genogram," 213.

6. Myron R. Chartier, "Family Spirituality," *Military Chaplains' Review* 17 (1998): 12.

7. Esther de Waal, "Family Spirituality," in *The Westminster Dictionary of Christian Spirituality*, ed. Gordon S. Wakefield (Philadelphia: Westminster, 1983), 146.

8. Henri J. M. Nouwen, "Spirituality and the Family," *Weavings: A Journal of the Christian Spiritual Life* 3/1 (1988): 6–12.

9. Ernest Boyer Jr., *Finding God at Home: Family Life as Spiritual Discipline* (San Francisco: HarperSanFrancisco, 1988), 57.

10. Kathleen R. Fischer, "Spirituality and the Aging Family: A Systems Perspective," *Journal of Religious Gerontology* 8/4 (1992): 12.

11. Mark H. Butler and James M. Harper, "The Divine Triangle: God in the Marital System of Religious Couples," *Family Process* 33 (1994): 279, emphasis in original.

12. Butler and Harper, "The Divine Triangle," 281.

13. See Edwin Friedman, *Generation to Generation: Family Process in Church and Synagogue* (New York: Guilford, 1985), 27ff.

14. John Welwood, "Intimate Relationship as Path," in *Spirituality and Couples: Heart and Soul in the Therapy Process*, ed. Barbara Jo Brothers (New York: Haworth, 1992), 27, emphasis in original.

9. DISCOVERING YOUR PURPOSE: EXPLORING VOCATION IN SHORT-TERM GROUP SPIRITUAL DIRECTION

1. These ideas are adapted from Lynn C. Bauman's books *A Handbook to Practical Wisdom: A Study Guide* (Telephone, Tex.: Praxis, n.d.), and *Foundations of Christian Spirituality: The Biblical Tradition* (Telephone, Tex.: Praxis, 2003), which are available at www.praxisofprayer.com.

2. These exercises are adapted from Marjorie Thompson's book *Soul Feast: An Invitation to the Christian Spiritual Life* (Louisville, Ky.: Westminster John Knox, 1995).

ANNOTATED BIBLIOGRAPHY

Allen, Joseph J. *Inner Way: Toward a Rebirth of Eastern Christian Spiritual Direction.* Reprint, Brookline, Mass.: Holy Cross Orthodox, 1999.
Written from the perspective of the Orthodox tradition. Establishes theological foundation for the practice of spiritual direction. Engages historical and psychological concerns.

Bakke, Jeannette A. *Holy Invitations: Exploring Spiritual Direction.* Grand Rapids: Baker, 2000.
Introductory text from a Protestant perspective. Distinguishes between spiritual direction and other types of pastoral care. Helpful discussion of the risks and benefits involved in spiritual direction.

Barry, William A., and William J. Connolly. *The Practice of Spiritual Direction.* San Francisco: HarperSanFrancisco, 1986.
A classic text in American spiritual direction, focused on preparing individuals to provide spiritual direction to others. Despite an out-of-date use of psychology, the book provides an excellent foundation for understanding and practicing the ministry of spiritual direction. Chapters focused on the relationship between director and directee are particularly helpful.

Conroy, Maureen. *The Discerning Heart: Discovering a Personal God.* Chicago: Loyola, 1993.
A thorough and accessible introduction to spiritual discernment in the Ignatian Rules for Discernment. Includes a number of practical questions and reflection exercises to help develop skill in discernment. Highly recommended.

Dougherty, Rose Mary. *Group Spiritual Direction: Community for Discernment.* New York: Paulist, 1995.
Useful guide to spiritual direction in a group context. Sensitive to a variety of traditions and approaches. Provides both a theological foundation for group direction and a practical guide for establishing and

facilitating such a group. Focused on fostering contemplative listening among participants.

Edwards, Tilden. *Spiritual Director, Spiritual Companion: Guide to Tending the Soul.* New York: Paulist, 2001.
  Basic text for directors and directees. Focused on understanding the soul and ways of knowing spiritual experience. Full of practical suggestions for nurturing spirituality. An appendix provides a model of a peer supervision group for spiritual directors.

Fischer, Kathleen. *Women at the Well: Feminist Perspectives on Spiritual Direction.* New York: Paulist, 1988.
  Focused on the dynamics of spiritual direction with women. Integrates feminist theology and psychology into the theory and practice of spiritual direction. Each chapter includes suggestions for prayer and reflection. Helpful chapters on power, violence, and anger. Recommended.

Gratton, Carolyn. *The Art of Spiritual Guidance: A Contemporary Approach to Growing in the Spirit.* New York: Crossroad, 1992.
  A thorough overview of the ministry of spiritual direction. Integrates psychology more effectively than any other text. Rooted theologically in a communal understanding of freedom, justice, and love. Includes helpful discussion of discernment. Recommended.

Guenther, Margaret. *Holy Listening: The Art of Spiritual Direction.* Cambridge, Mass.: Cowley, 1992.
  Warm, sensitive, and wise introduction to spiritual direction in the Anglican tradition. Includes a chapter on special issues encountered in spiritual direction with women. Solid theological grounding. Recommended.

Jeff, Gordon. *Spiritual Direction for Every Christian.* London: SPCK, 1987.
  Practical, down-to-earth guide. Presents spiritual direction as a part of every Christian's vocation rather than a specialized ministry. Includes helpful discussions of how to conduct a first session, resources to draw on in the course of spiritual direction, and spiritual retreats.

Jones, Alan. *Exploring Spiritual Direction.* 1982. Reprint, Cambridge, Mass.: Cowley, 1999.
  Reprint (with a new foreword) of a pioneering work in contemporary spiritual direction. Establishes Christian friendship as a foundation for the practice of spiritual direction. An introductory text.

Kelsey, Morton. *Companions on the Inner Way: The Art of Spiritual Guidance.* 2nd ed. New York: Crossroad, 1996.
 Looks at spiritual friendship from the perspective of Anglican theology and Jungian psychology. Sensitive to postmodern assumptions that permeate North American culture. Helpful exploration of the nature of religious experience.

Leech, Kenneth. *Soul Friend: An Invitation to Spiritual Direction.* With an introduction by Henri Nouwen. 1977. Reprint, San Francisco: Harper-Collins, 1980.
 Introductory text focused on spiritual direction as guidance in the life of prayer. Extensive comparison of spiritual direction to psychotherapy. A pioneering text.

Liebert, Elizabeth. *Changing Life Patterns: Adult Development in Spiritual Direction.* Expanded ed. St. Louis: Chalice, 2000.
 Integrates Christian traditions of spiritual direction with developmental psychology. Includes attention to congregational context of spiritual direction.

May, Gerald G. *Care of Mind, Care of Spirit: Psychiatric Dimensions of Spiritual Direction.* San Francisco: Harper & Row, 1982.
 Explores spiritual direction from a psychiatric perspective. Not an introductory text.

Ruffing, Janet. *Spiritual Direction: Beyond the Beginnings.* New York: Paulist, 2000.
 Focused on advanced themes, issues, and dynamics that occur in the lives of directees and in the practice of spiritual direction. Uses narrative theory to provide an understanding of the direction process. Recommended.

Stairs, Jean. *Listening for the Soul: Pastoral Care and Spiritual Direction.* Minneapolis: Fortress Press, 2000.
 Explores intersection of spiritual direction and pastoral care in the congregational context. Includes a chapter on caring for the souls of children.

Vest, Norvene, ed. *Still Listening: New Horizons in Spiritual Direction.* Harrisburg, Pa.: Morehouse, 2000.
 An edited volume providing insight for the practice of spiritual direction with members of specific populations, including abused people, the poor, gay and lesbian people, addicts, and the dying.

BIBLIOGRAPHY OF WEB RESOURCES

http://www.anamchara.com

An interfaith website devoted to the Celtic tradition of spiritual friendship. Includes book reviews, resources for mysticism, author and musician interviews, and links to other interesting sites.

http://www.aril.org

Maintained by the nonprofit Association for Religion and Intellectual Life, this is the website of the magazine *CrossCurrents*. The site includes article texts, links to other religion and spirituality websites, and more.

http://www.beliefnet.com

A multifaith e-community. Includes columnists, sacred texts, spiritual assessment tools, religious news, book reviews, and other resources. Interesting, captivating, and engaging. Will send daily emails on a variety of subjects.

http://www.christdesert.org

The Monastery of Christ in the Desert in Abiquiu, New Mexico. Classic monastic understandings of spirituality.

http://www.creighton.edu/CollaborativeMinistry/online.html

An online ministry of Creighton University in Omaha, Nebraska, this website includes daily reflections, an online retreat, the stations of the cross, and helpful content about spirituality.

http://www.elca.org

The Evangelical Lutheran Church in America. Check out the Resources section. (This is usually a good thing to do at any site.)

http://www.faithandvalues.com

Includes materials from the spiritual traditions of Christianity and Judaism. Explores the intersection of faith and ethical decision-making in the realms of family life, politics, academia, and daily life. Excellent resource on a variety of subjects related to spirituality.

http://www.gracecathedral.org
The motto of this site is "reconnecting your spirit without disconnecting your mind." Hosted by the Episcopal cathedral of San Francisco, the site includes articles, audio and video links, and information on walking the labyrinth as a spiritual practice. Content is always changing, so visit often.

http://www.iona.org.uk
The Iona Community is a Celtic community that has some really useful resources for worship and spirituality.

http://www.jesuit.ie/livingspace
Resources for prayer, scripture, and daily life maintained by the Irish Jesuits. Content usually changes weekly.

http://www.jesuit.ie/prayer
Maintained by the Irish Jesuits, this site leads you through a ten-minute *lectio divina* on your computer screen, using a daily lectionary. Significant on-screen guidance provided for those who appreciate it. This site will quickly become a daily destination. Users of AdvantGo can download the daily prayers to a personal digital assistant.

http://www.osb.org
The website of the Order of Saint Benedict.

http://www.pcusa.org/spiritualformation
Office of Spiritual Formation for the Presbyterian Church (USA). Includes online journal, resources, and helpful links.

http://www.retreatsintl.org
Retreats International website. Includes information on types of retreats and a directory of retreat centers. Also supports the Institute for Adult Spiritual Renewal.

http://www.science-spirit.org
A website (and magazine, *Science & Spirit*) exploring how science and religion can work together to address issues of contemporary concern. Site features articles, departments, and web exclusives.

http://www.sdiworld.org

The website of Spiritual Directors International, a professional organization for spiritual directors. Includes helpful content about spiritual direction, a directory of training programs, and an index of the organization's peer-reviewed journal.

http://www.spiritualityhealth.com

Addressing the intersection of spirituality and health, this website offers significant, ever-changing content to explore a variety of spiritual topics, practices, and disciplines. Online courses, email retreats, and "spiritual literacy" modules are particularly helpful.

http://www.taize.fr/en/index.htm

The English-language version of the website for the Taizé Community in France. Lots of resources; see especially the Prayer and Song link.

http://www.ucc.org

The website of the United Church of Christ. The Forums tab includes an online prayer chapel and other helpful content.

http://www.upperroom.org

The web presence of Upper Room Ministries, this site includes resources for personal spirituality, daily devotionals, access to Upper Room publications, a prayer center, an online chapel, and other helpful options.

http://www.wccm.org

Online headquarters of the World Community for Christian Meditation. Associated with the Order of Saint Benedict. Interviews with spiritual teachers and reflections for the seasons of the church year.

http://www.worldprayers.org

A multicultural prayer collective featuring prayers from spiritual traditions all over the world. Inspiring.

INDEX

Allen, Joseph, 10n8, 54n3, 56n5
Anderson, Douglas A., 96n2
Anderson, Harlene, 17n2, 18, 18n3, 18n4, 23, 23n18
appropriate knowing, 24, 32, 71, 78

Bakke, Jeannette, 6, 6n3
Barry, William A., 4, 5, 44, 44n3
Bauman, Lynn, 24n20, 81n12, 111n1
Benedict, Rule of, 5
Bondi, Roberta, 73, 73n3
Box, Hubert S., 11
Boyer, Ernest Jr., 99, 100n9, 101
brief pastoral counseling, 27n1
    principles of, 28–34
    techniques of, 52–68
Butler, Mark, 105, 105nn11–12

Capps, Donald, 21, 21n9
Chartier, Myron R., 99n6
Chrysostom, John, 10
Coakley, Sarah, 22–23, 22nn11–16, 23n17
Cockburn, Jack, 27n2
Coelho, Marcy C., 29n4
compliments, 47–48, 65–67
confession, 5, 70, 75–76, 104
Connolly, William, 4, 5n2, 29, 29n4, 44, 44n3
Conroy, Maureen, 85n1, 86n5, 87, 87n8

consolation, spiritual, 87–90
contemplative space, 70–72
Culligan, Kevin G., 10, 10n12

deconstruction, 61–63
depression, 89–90
desolation, spiritual, 67, 87–90
de Waal, Esther, 56n5, 87n7
differentiation, 105
discernment of thoughts, 5, 74
discernment, spiritual, 84–94
disclosure of thoughts, 5, 74, 75
disposition, 54, 55, 73
Driskill, Joseph, 78, 78n9
Dubay, Thomas, 6n5, 39n1
Duncombe, David, 85, 85n3
Dunn, Adriana Balguer, 97n4

ecomaps, 96, 98–99
Edwards, Tilden, 4n1
exceptions, 29–30, 60–61

Fischer, Kathleen R., 103n10
Foster, Richard, 75–76, 76nn7–8
Fowler, James, 13, 13n1
Frame, Marsha Wiggins, 97, 97n4, 98n5
Friedman, Edwin, 105n13

genograms, 96, 97–98
Giblin, Paul, 95, 95n1
goals in spiritual direction, 31–32, 44–47, 90